The NO-NONSENSE GUIDE to
WORLD HEALTH

'Publishers have created lists of short books that discuss the questions that your average [electoral] candidate will only ever touch if armed with a slogan and a soundbite. Together [such books] hint at a resurgence of the grand educational tradition... Closest to the hot headline issues are *The No-Nonsense Guides*. These target those topics that a large army of voters care about, but that politicos evade. Arguments, figures and documents combine to prove that good journalism is far too important to be left to (most) journalists.'

Boyd Tonkin,
The Independent,
London

About the author
Shereen Usdin is a South African medical doctor with a Masters in Public Health from Harvard University. She was a 2004 Shoprite-Checkers/SABC Woman of the Year and named one of the Gordon Institute of Business Science's 2006 Social Entrepreneurs of the Year. She is a Senior Executive at the Soul City Institute for Health and Development Communication and sits on South Africa's Presidential Working Group on Women. She writes in her personal capacity.

Acknowledgements
Jonathan Berger, Professor Sharon Fonn, Professor Rachel Jewkes, Priya Naidu, Associate Professor Rafael Obregon, Mohau Pheko, Lebo Ramafoko, Professor David Sanders, Sarah Sexton, Scott Sinclair, Karen, Martine, Renee and Ros Usdin, Haroon Wadee and Troth Wells for their precious time and good advice. And my daughter Romy for her precious presence.

Other titles in the series
The No-Nonsense Guide to Animal Rights
The No-Nonsense Guide to Climate Change
The No-Nonsense Guide to Conflict and Peace
The No-Nonsense Guide to Fair Trade
The No-Nonsense Guide to Globalization
The No-Nonsense Guide to Human Rights
The No-Nonsense Guide to International Development
The No-Nonsense Guide to Islam
The No-Nonsense Guide to Science
The No-Nonsense Guide to Sexual Diversity
The No-Nonsense Guide to Tourism
The No-Nonsense Guide to World History
The No-Nonsense Guide to World Poverty

About the New Internationalist
The **New Internationalist** is an independent not-for-profit publishing co-operative. Our mission is to report on issues of global justice. We publish informative current affairs and popular reference titles, complemented by world food, photography and gift books as well as calendars, diaries, maps and posters – all with a global justice world view.

If you like this *No-Nonsense Guide* you'll also love the **New Internationalist** magazine. Each month it takes a different subject such as *Trade Justice*, *Nuclear Power* or *Iraq*, exploring and explaining the issues in a concise way; the magazine is full of photos, charts and graphs as well as music, film and book reviews, country profiles, interviews and news.

To find out more about the **New Internationalist**, visit our website at
www.newint.org

The NO-NONSENSE GUIDE to
WORLD HEALTH

Shereen Usdin

The No-Nonsense Guide to World Health
First published in the UK in 2007 by
New Internationalist™ Publications Ltd
Oxford OX4 1BW, UK
www.newint.org
New Internationalist is a registered trade mark.

Series editor: Troth Wells
Design by New Internationalist Publications Ltd.

 Printed on recycled paper by T J Press International, Cornwall, UK
who hold environmental accreditation ISO 14001.

Cover image: Sleeping sickness screening, Sudan.
© Sven Torfinn/Panos Pictures.

British Library Cataloguing-in-Publication Data.
A catalogue record for this book is available from the British Library.

Library of Congress Cataloguing-in-Publication Data.
A catalogue for this book is available from the Library of Congress.

ISBN 978-1-904456-65-0

Foreword

AT THE DAWN of the 21st century we have the wherewithal, more than ever before, to secure a life of health and wellbeing for each and every citizen of this earth. And yet millions of people still die every day from preventable diseases such as HIV/AIDS, TB, diarrhea, malaria and measles. The list is long.

Over the last 5 years, more than 40 million Africans alone died deaths that could have been averted if we were only committed to doing so. This number surpasses the total deaths from all modern African and global conflicts including the two world wars. It is roughly the equivalent of the combined population of Africa's 10 least populous countries. The total number of deaths *worldwide* that result from preventable diseases is almost beyond our capacity to imagine.

How is it possible that in a world with unparalleled wealth, so many people die of diseases that have their roots in grueling, demeaning, dehumanizing poverty?

Poverty has many causes but the current inequities are in large part due to a globalizing economy that is gathering wealth at the expense of the poor. Trade has the potential to lift millions of poor people around the world out of poverty but currently it is doing the opposite. Unfair trade rules are allowing the rich to get richer, while the poor are getting poorer. Today, more than half the population of Africa lives on less than a dollar a day.

The citizens of many countries that have thrown off the shackles of colonialism had great hopes for freedom. But freedom is nothing if it does not translate into electricity; clean water; a safe place to live; a job that pays a living wage; schools for one's children and access to health care.

At the moment wealthy nations spend billions on weapons when a fraction of the world's military budgets would eradicate poverty and provide basic needs from food to clean water for everyone. If the wealthy nations were really committed to improving the lives of the poorer nations we could end poverty and in doing so reduce the tragic death toll from poverty-related diseases.

The fact that so many people are poor and live in an unequal world creates a crisis that affects us all. Poverty not only gives rise to diseases that can spread around the globe, it also jeopardizes national economies and endangers social and political security. As humans, we are bound together and ultimately we will sink or swim together.

My dream is that one day my children will wake up and realize that they are members of one global family. A family that cares for one another.

It is my hope that every child has a decent chance of survival, that every child can have access to an adequate education and health care. The spin-off for individual countries and ultimately for the entire world would be tremendous.

We must do something because it is the logic of being human. We cannot be human on our own: we can be human only together.

Shereen Usdin's *No-Nonsense Guide to World Health* is premised on this belief – that without social justice, a life of health and dignity for all the world's people cannot be fully realized.

Archbishop Emeritus Desmond Tutu
Nobel Peace Prize Laureate

CONTENTS

Introduction

IN 1981, AS a young medical student at the University of the Witwatersrand in Johannesburg, I attended a conference called 'Apartheid and Health: History of the Main Complaint'. It joined many dots for me at a time in South Africa when there was little that made sense.

All good doctors begin examinations by asking about 'the history of the main complaint'. This precedes the physical examination and is designed to get to the bottom of the problem. 'Where is the pain, when did it start, what makes it worse, what makes it better?' And so on. A diagnosis follows and treatment is prescribed.

The 'Apartheid and Health' conference challenged us to go beyond this history and ask questions that would get to the root cause of disease and death under apartheid.

This questioning would reveal the history of a man whose main complaint was a lingering cough with night sweats and chest pain. The disease was TB but the root cause was his life as a miner exposed to the bacillus while extracting the gold South Africa is famous for. Denied the vote under apartheid, black South Africans were made citizens of arid homelands in far-flung areas. A pool of labor for White South Africa, but unable to live there permanently, people became migrants in their own country. Living in squalid, overcrowded single-sex hostels, lack of decent food and poor working conditions made the miner an easy target for infection.

This interpretation of the history of the main complaint has resonated with many others. My work as a doctor only served to solidify the diagnosis that ill health is inextricably linked to poverty and inequity for which social justice is the cure.

This book was written in the heat of a Johannesburg summer with mosquitoes buzzing around my sleeping child. I imagined what it would be like to be a parent in an endemic malaria area. It would be hard to have a good night's sleep. And yet, despite a million children dying every year from malaria, the world sleeps.

This book examines what we are sleeping through. It looks at the political economy of health in today's world. It hopes to answer why in this day and age, where there is so much wealth, there is also so much suffering.

Every attempt has been made to reflect the terrain accurately but new developments on the global health landscape have arisen even in the course of writing this book. The G8 group of richest countries is soon to meet again and new commitments will be made. Or maybe not.

It is an enormous field to traverse and there is not enough space in this book to do it full justice. Many important health-related areas are missing – war and other complex humanitarian emergencies, disability, youth, education, and much else. Some issues, reduced to paragraphs here, are the subject of tomes. The scope of the problem is disheartening on many levels.

But at the same time there is cause for optimism. Not so long ago, books suggesting 'another world is possible' were relegated to shelves alongside dusty copies of *Das Kapital*. Nowadays this view is increasingly mainstream. People are seeing the impact of the current world order all around them. With this has come an acknowledgement that the treatment for the main complaint is a commitment to social justice and the universality of human rights.

Shereen Usdin
Johannesburg, South Africa

1 No 'Health for All' by the 21st century

'Modern high-tech warfare is designed to remove physical contact: dropping bombs from 50,000 ft ensures that one does not "feel" what one does. Modern economic management is similar: from one's luxury hotel, one can callously impose policies about which one would think twice if one knew the people whose lives one was destroying.'

Joseph Stiglitz, former World Bank Chief Economist and Nobel Laureate in Economics, 2001.[1]

Spectacular gains in life expectancy have taken place but the benefits have been unevenly distributed. Today's world is beset with inequities exacting an enormous toll on health. The causes go way back but they have been deepened by macroeconomic policies imposed over the last few decades on the South. Serving the interests of the North they are in large part why WHO's clarion call of 'Health For All by the Year 2000' remains a lofty dream.

If an alien were to land on earth today it would have a hard time explaining things to the mothership. It would flash back photographs of Citizen X, sipping mineral water in his luxury penthouse, followed by Citizen Y's mother collecting water from a stagnant stream.[i]

Today, 1.1 billion people do not have access to adequate amounts of safe water and 2.6 billion lack basic sanitation,[2] making hygiene impossible. Together they make Citizen Y vulnerable to a host of infections. She could be one of the 1.5 million children who die each year from diarrhea because of this.[3] Because no

---

i In UNICEF-supported research in 23 countries more than a fifth of households surveyed spend more than an hour per trip to collect water and in areas with taps, irregular or interrupted supplies cause delays of hours.

health education ever reached her village, her mother does not know about lifesaving oral rehydration therapy. The clinic is too far to walk to and there is no money to pay for transport or the clinic visit.

If Citizen Y recovers, her chances of making it beyond her fifth birthday are slim. If infections don't kill her, they could leave her blind or undernourished in her critical developmental years, with compromised physical and cognitive functioning. Disadvantaged at school, if she gets to go, what chance does she stand to perform well, graduate, get a job and escape the poverty she was born into? Poverty begets ill-health which begets poverty.

The alien would report that there is some trouble in paradise – living high on the hog makes Citizen X vulnerable to chronic diseases.[ii] But when he has his heart attack at 70 he will be rushed to a state-of-the-art hospital where the best medical team will work wonders.

We live in an era where spectacular things are possible. We've mapped the Human Genome, grown organ tissue from embryonic stem cells and may be close to cloning a human being. We can replace the human heart with an artificial one and do intricate surgery via computer. These are the days of 'miracles and wonder'. But this offers little relief from the grinding poverty and ill-health experienced by almost half the world. They are the 2.8 billion people who live on less than $2 per day. In Ethiopia they are called *wuha anfari* – 'those who cook water'.

Spectacular gains, spectacular inequity

Our hunter-gathering ancestors roamed the earth for 25 years on average. Major gains were only made in the mid-19th century and by the 1950s we were

ii Ironically chronic diseases are also on the rise amongst the poor (see Chapter 6).

roaming on average for about 20 to 30 years more. Improvements in socio-economic conditions with better living standards (including water and sanitation provision) and nutrition were largely responsible for the dramatic gains in life expectancy in the mid-19th century. While these gains pre-dated larger public health interventions including oral rehydration therapy and immunization, some argue that the role of these technological interventions is understated.

Life expectancy shot up in the last half of the 20th century, spiking today at 80 years in some parts of the world.[4] Continuing improvements in socio-economic conditions and better medical interventions, notably treatment of infections and prevention and control of non-communicable diseases such as diabetes and cardiovascular disease, have been largely responsible for gains post-1950.

While the majority of the world is better off today than a century ago, these gains have been unequally distributed both between and within countries. In some parts of the world you would be lucky to make it to 40. Life expectancies have decreased in sub-Saharan Africa (largely because of HIV) and in the former Soviet Union (largely because of social disruption, increased poverty and the collapse of social services). In industrialized countries only 1 in 28,000 women will die from causes related to childbearing, while in sub-Saharan Africa the risk is 1 in 16. In wealthy Australia there is a 20-year gap in life expectancy

What's in a name?

Terminology describing countries' varying degrees of 'development' is highly contested. This book tends to use 'North' and 'South', 'Western' and 'Majority World', 'rich' and 'poor', although they are all imperfect. For example, in 1990, the *Fortune* 500 included 19 transnational companies from the South. This rose to 57 in 2006. Journalist Thebe Mabanga quips: 'World domination is now as likely to be plotted from an air-conditioned office in Mumbai as it is from New York'.

Inequitable and iniquitous

According to the UN Millennium Project's Jeffrey Sachs the gap between rich and poor nations has been widening steadily from 12-fold in 1961, to 30-fold in 1997 with simultaneous disparities in life expectancy and infant mortality rates between and within countries.

While under-5 mortality rates (the number of children dying under 5 years per 1,000 live births per year) declined overall, the rate of decline differed. Between 1990 and 2002 rates declined by 81 per cent in industrialized countries, 60 per cent in developing and 44 per cent in the poorest countries. This decline has stagnated and is reversing in some countries, particularly in Africa.

Under-5 mortality rates by country income level (per 1,000 live births)

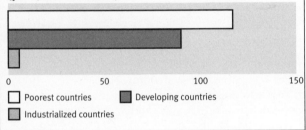

Legend:
- ☐ Poorest countries
- ■ Developing countries
- ■ Industrialized countries

between Aboriginals and the Australian average. Premature death in African-American men is 90 per cent higher than in whites.[5]

According to UNICEF global access to water increased from 78 to 83 per cent between 1990 and 2004. But this masks wide inter- and intra-country disparities particularly between urban and rural communities. In West/Central Africa for example, about 49 million people living in urban areas gained access to improved drinking-water sources during this period, but only 26 million people living in rural areas did so. In some countries the discrepancies are very high. For example, in Mongolia, 87 per cent of urban dwellers have access to safe water supplies while only 30 per cent of rural dwellers do.

Today's global averages look less rosy when

disaggregated by gender, race, geographical location or bank balance. These factors, plus others, are referred to as 'the socio-economic determinants' of health. Reflecting differing levels of social privilege, they determine your exposure to risk, your access to life opportunities and resources (including safe water and sanitation, education, and health services). They determine how long and how healthily you live.

It is no surprise that absolute deprivation has negative health outcomes. This is why more than 10 million children die of hunger and preventable diseases every year – astoundingly, one every three seconds. They die largely from a few poverty-related conditions: pneumonia, diarrhea-related diseases, malaria, measles, HIV/AIDS, under-nutrition and neonatal conditions. Most of these deaths happen in the South.

But inequality *per se* within societies is also thought to result in negative outcomes through perceptions of social deprivation, even when relatively small. Lack of social cohesion and inadequate political support for redistributive policies in such societies are also thought to be responsible.

In fact poorer countries with less inequity often have equal or better health measures than wealthy countries with large disparities. For example, Sri Lanka and India's Kerala state are both poor, but have limited income variation and invested heavily in redistributive, pro-equity policies. Basic curative and preventive health services were combined with strategies to ensure land reform, universal access to housing, education (emphasizing gender equity), subsidized school transport and nutrition, water, sanitation and extensive social safety nets.

Kerala's per capita income is about a hundredth that of wealthier countries. It spends $28 per capita on health compared to the US which spends $3,925. But life expectancies of 76 for women and 74 for men

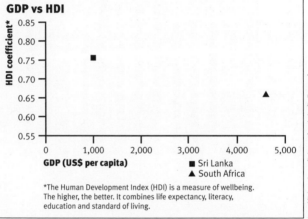

Economic growth and good health are not automatically synonymous

Once a minimum per capita income is achieved, education and other socio-political investments have greater health impacts than economic growth.* This is why poorer countries with less inequality often score better on health measures than wealthy counterparts with greater inequality. Sri Lanka for example scores higher on the Human Development Index* than South Africa which has a 4-fold higher per capita GDP but is one of the world's most unequal countries.

*R Beaglehole, R Bonita, *Public Health at the Crossroads: Achievements and Prospects* (Cambridge University Press, 2004).

GDP vs HDI

HDI coefficient*

0.85
0.80
0.75
0.70
0.65
0.60
0.55

0   1,000   2,000   3,000   4,000   5,000

GDP (US$ per capita)   ■ Sri Lanka   ▲ South Africa

*The Human Development Index (HDI) is a measure of wellbeing. The higher, the better. It combines life expectancy, literacy, education and standard of living.

http://hdr.undp.org/hdr2006/statistics/indicators/

are roughly on par with those in the US (80 and 74 years respectively).[6] Infant Mortality Rates (IMR) in Kerala at 14 per 1,000 live births are close to the US average rates (7 per 1,000). But citizens of Kerala fare better than African-Americans whose IMRs are well below the US average. They also fare better than those in equally poor parts of India where average IMRs are 68 per 1,000.

Health equity means 'any group of individuals defined by age, gender, race-ethnicity, class or residence is able to achieve its full health potential.'[7] Addressing

Beneath the rosy surface

According to UNICEF, global access to water increased from 78 per cent in 1990 to 83 per cent in 2004. But this masks wide inter- and intra-country disparities, particularly between urban and rural communities. One inequity leads to another – studies show that girls miss days of learning during their menstrual periods or drop out of school entirely as a result of lack of privacy, where schools lack separate water and sanitation facilities for them.

Urban-rural differences in access to water supply

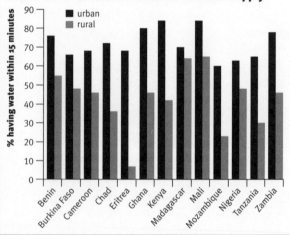

ORC Macro, 2007. MEASURE DHS STATcompiler. http://www.measuredhs.com, March 16 2007.

poverty and inequity is unequivocally the greatest challenge facing public health in the 21st century.

So how did it get to be this way?

Simply put, the haves have, because everyone else has not. Since the days when sea-faring adventurers set forth to pillage and plunder, the world has been a bargain bin for wealthy nations. For the vanquished, life was cheap and full of hardship. Entire civilizations were wiped out. Later forms of colonialism were equally cruel. In the 1890s, Cecil John Rhodes, mining magnate and politician in South Africa, said shamelessly: 'We must find new lands from which we can easily obtain raw materials and at the same time exploit the cheap slave labor that is available from the natives in the colonies. The colonies [will] also provide a dumping ground for the surplus goods produced in our factories'.[8] By the mid-20th century, colonial powers were still sucking countries dry of resources, expropriating land from peasants for large-scale cultivation to feed the empires and lowering local food production. People were worked to death or spat out when they were sick and dying. Over a century later, modern forms of colonialism, dressed in the rhetoric of 'the free market' are doing the same. But more on that later.

While the health of the colonized deteriorated, two tiers of health services prevailed – quality services for the élites and third-rate care for the rest. Services were based in urban areas, and largely curative in nature.

In 1948, in the idealistic aftermath of the Second World War, the United Nations (UN) was born, and with it came global acknowledgements of health as a human right linked inextricably to social and economic justice. The Universal Declaration of Human Rights held that 'Everyone has the right to a standard of living adequate for the health and well-being of himself and of his family, including food, clothing, housing and medical care and necessary social services.' The 1966 International Covenant on Economic, Social and

The right to health

'General Comment 14', added to the UN's International Covenant on Social, Economic and Cultural Rights in 2000, states that the right to health is 'an inclusive right extending not only to timely and appropriate health care, but also to the underlying determinants of health, such as access to safe and potable water and adequate sanitation, an adequate supply of safe food, nutrition and housing, healthy occupational and environmental conditions and access to health-related education and information, including on sexual and reproductive health'.

Adapted from the Harvard Public Health Review Spring 2005.

If there was no poverty...

During the 1980s, the richest 1 per cent in the US increased their share of the country's wealth from 31 to 37 per cent. Yet in 1991 almost one-fifth of mortality in people between ages 25 to 74 was due to poverty.

Poverty's impact on health

The Harvard Public Health Disparities Geocoding Project team calculated what would happen to the number of cases in their study if everyone faced the same risk as people who were living in areas where fewer than five per cent of residents were impoverished.

% of cases that would not have occurred

Homicides and legal interventions	72.9
Syphilis	72.7
Gonorrhea	71.0
Weapons injuries	70.4
Childhood lead poisoning	69.8
Tuberculosis	56.5
Chlamydia	55.5
HIV/AIDS deaths	54.4
Low birth weight (<2,500g)	24.2
Premature mortality (death before age 65)	22.5

Cultural Rights (and more recent additions) elaborated on this even further (see box: The right to health p17). The World Health Organization (WHO) was established as the UN's specialized health agency to serve as the world's 'health conscience' and safeguard this inalienable right to health. It defined health as a state of wellbeing, not simply the absence of disease.

The rise of Primary Health Care (PHC)

Postcolonial concerns for health and social justice varied. In some countries the oppressor simply became 'home-grown'. Inequities continued and even intensified. Many countries continued to follow the colonizers' medical model of health care with costly urban hospitals and 'doctors as God'. For others, radical change was in the air. With oppression came a strong consciousness of the link between poor health and social injustice. Countries such as Mozambique and Tanzania trail-blazed a people-centered model of development. Bringing health to the people was seen as an act of liberation. In 1977 the Frelimo Government in Mozambique stated its objective to make 'each citizen a sanitary agent and to arm and organize the people to defend themselves and their health'.[9] China's famous 'barefoot doctors' were villagers trained to provide basic health care in their own communities.

These efforts influenced global trends and in 1978, at WHO's International Conference on Primary Health Care (PHC) in Alma Ata (now Almaty), Kazakhstan, member countries committed to this approach. PHC was more than just providing basic services. It was a revolutionary concept with social justice at its core. Eradicating inequity was to be a global priority. Services would provide integrated basic preventive, curative and rehabilitative care close to where people lived. More complex problems would be referred to the next level of health service. PHC services would work closely with health-related sectors responsible for education, safe water and sanitation and food security. In this way, addressing the socio-economic determinants of health would be part of the PHC equation. Communities would be active participants in the entire process.

At Alma Ata, governments committed to achieving 'Health For All by the Year 2000' with PHC as a central strategy. It was a time of great optimism and 'another world' seemed possible.

The fall of Primary Health Care

But the heady idealism soon faded in the 1980s as the right to health was systematically eroded. While some countries like Sri Lanka remained steadfast, in most PHC was reduced to rhetoric and lip-service.

One reason for this was that influential donors

viewed it as too costly. They advocated a whittled down package of interventions and 'selective primary health care' became the new buzzword. It was derided almost immediately by critics as 'Health for *Some* by the Year 2000'.

Many packages were also vertically applied, a trend which continues to dominate the health landscape today. Unlike comprehensive, integrated PHC which ensures a one-stop shop for a wide spectrum of essential health care services, selective, vertical programs are run as separate silos. Many vertical programs are single-disease focused, to the exclusion, and at the cost of, other equally important health needs. Mass immunization drives are one such example. They have made significant inroads in child health. But because of their narrow focus, broader strategies to improve

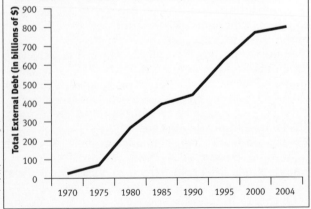

Funny money – growing debt

Under structural adjustment programs (SAPs), debt repayment got completely out of hand. Nigeria for example borrowed $5 billion in 1986, paid back $16 billion but absurdly now owes $32 billion. By the late 1990s, debt in the South amounted to $3,000 billion.

Total Latin American and Caribbean external debt

USAID; http://qesdb.usaid.gov/

health get neglected, including the strengthening of the health system as a whole.

Some believe governments and international donors found the concept of community control over health care delivery too revolutionary. It certainly held little appeal for the medical establishment. Sadly too, some communities associated quality care with big hospitals and bypassed the PHC service. Because PHC was often under-funded, it reinforced the view of a second-rate service.[10]

Many post-independence governments were committed to development and experienced impressive average annual growth. But others were corrupt and repressive, lining the pockets of their élites instead of investing in the health of their citizenry. This hardly helped generate funds or political will for PHC.

Critically, the Alma Ata strategy was predicated on a New International Economic Order that never materialized. It was presumed money would be diverted from militarization but in many areas wars escalated. Simultaneously macro-economic forces that led to spiraling debt, fiscal austerity measures and market-driven health sector reforms deepened inequities and devastated the public sector. This was perhaps the greatest reason for the failure of PHC.

Macro-economic mayhem

Things started to go awry across Africa, Latin America and Asia, when the Organization of Petroleum Exporting Countries (OPEC) massively increased the price of petroleum. A surplus of 'petrodollars' ended up in commercial banks in the West. These banks looked to increase lending to the South which now desperately needed money to pay its fuel bills and fund development. The oil crisis plunged the North into recession. Interest rate hikes and later the devaluation of the dollar shot Southern debt into the stratosphere.

Some of this debt was also owed to the World Bank.[iii] While the Bank's original job was to assist countries to rebuild themselves post-World War Two, its mandate soon shifted as the West recovered. It began to loan money to newly independent countries, largely to build infrastructure capacity.

Much debt owed is considered 'odious', that is, lent knowingly by Western bankers to repressive, corrupt dictators. The astronomical accumulation of wealth by these leaders at the expense of their citizens is legendary. Former Philippines' president Ferdinand Marcos stole around $10 billion. Some ended up on his well-heeled wife Imelda, who insisted she had '1,060 pairs of shoes, not 3,000'. Loans also propped up dictators to serve the goals of the Cold War. Millions went to 'development' projects, which were often outright scams. Past rulers of Nigeria stole or misused some £220 billion/$400 billion. Two thirds of its 130 million citizens now live in abject poverty. Citizens who suffered under these regimes are again victimized through payment of debt not of their making. Nicaragua's odious debt is over five times the country's total GDP.

Capital flight from private investors into Western bank accounts, often a mechanism for tax evasion, also lost huge amounts available to governments for development. Between 1976 and 1984, for example, Argentina, Brazil, Mexico, the Philippines and Venezuela lost between $55 billion and $132 billion because of this. During this period, debt in those countries increased by a total of $243 billion.[11]

As economies were collapsing under the debt burden they were forced to enter into loan agreements with the IMF. Loans from the IMF and World Bank were

iii The World Bank is one of three international bodies referred to as the Bretton Woods Institutions. The others are the International Monetary Fund (IMF) and the General Agreement on Tariffs and Trade (GATT). They were established at a post-war conference in Bretton Woods in 1944 to set out the rules for a stable post-war global economy. GATT subsequently became the World Trade Organization (WTO).

contingent upon the adoption of fiscal austerity measures which later became known as 'structural adjustment programs' (SAPs). Measures included the rapid privatization of state enterprises and liberalization of trade and investment through the deregulation of financial markets. This included reduced corporate tax and labor controls and the removal of tariffs and quotas (as barriers to trade). Subsidies for basic foodstuffs were removed and social spending cut in essential services such as education, health, housing, water and sanitation. In the health sector, cost-recovery strategies such as user-fees were instituted.

While the North continued to subsidize its producers, the South was expected to open markets to international investors and cut their own subsidies. This made it impossible to compete and these unfair terms of trade persist up to today. Primary exports dwindled. Investors ousted local production to make way for export crops. People lost jobs and literally starved. According to the Food and Agriculture Organization (FAO) between 1992 and 2000, at the height of SAPs, the number of hungry people increased by almost 60 million.

The rationale behind SAPs, with its downsizing of the state and its market liberalization, was to free up public funds and to attract foreign currency to repay debt and grow the economy. The assumption was that, as the economic metaphor goes, 'the rising tide will lift all boats'. Trade would drive growth and growth would drive development. Wealth would trickle down to uplift the poor. Government 'interference' in the markets would discourage foreign investment. But in most instances, only the bigger boats floated and without state regulation, it became apparent that wealth does not trickle.

Jobs were lost and wages plummeted. In countries like Tanzania, real wages have fallen by 70 per cent since 1986.[12] Co-payments for health care and other public services meant the poor had to pay for essential care. Hard choices had to be made between food,

No 'Health for All' by the 21st century

Out of pocket

The trends in India mirror the global picture. With increasing privatization into the 21st century, the cost of health care falls on those least able to afford it. In many countries it consumes most of the household budget. Serious illness can bankrupt households worldwide and according to WHO pushes about 100 million people into poverty each year. Oxfam maintains that in Zambia, where almost 60 per cent of the population lives on a monthly income of less than $18, it costs $8-10 to treat one episode of pneumonia.

Share of entities in total health spending in India during 2001-2002

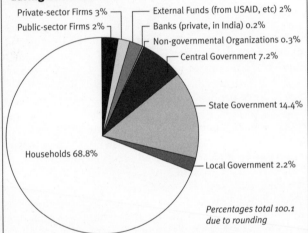

Private-sector Firms 3%
Public-sector Firms 2%
External Funds (from USAID, etc) 2%
Banks (private, in India) 0.2%
Non-governmental Organizations 0.3%
Central Government 7.2%
State Government 14.4%
Households 68.8%
Local Government 2.2%

Percentages total 100.1 due to rounding

Only about one-fourth of India's health dollars came from the government in 2001-02, while more than 70 per cent came from private sources, mainly citizens' pockets. Because those who use the national health system suffer long waits and substandard care, even the very poor turn instead to the large private sector of clinics and hospitals. Lacking health insurance, many families are overburdened – even bankrupted – by medical expenses.

school or health. Under SAPs, desperate families sold off livestock and other valuable assets to pay for healthcare. Children left school. Inequity increased on all fronts. Women were disproportionately affected (see Chapter 4). Usage of health services dropped with catastrophic results. When President Museveni of Uganda ended user-fees in 2001, attendance at clinics soared by 50 to 100 per cent.

Slashing health budgets resulted in poorly maintained and equipped health services with weak procurement and distribution of medicines and supplies. As a result, those who made it to the health services were met with supply shortages from drugs and bandages to health workers. Shrinking salaries forced skilled personnel out of the public sector or encouraged corruption, poor morale and patient abuse.

Debt continued to spiral with interest piling up on interest. By the late 1980s poverty was getting worse. Health systems had collapsed and reforms had all but destroyed social services and safety nets.

All this came with a heavy price on health. With soaring IMRs UNICEF, supported by WHO, devised a package of 'selective PHC' dubbed 'GOBI-FFF'[iv] to maximize health benefits for children. It fed into acrimonious debate within the international health arena on the value of selective and vertical programs. Their proponents were accused of 'selling out' PHC.

Increasingly beholden to donors and the IMF/World Bank, countries' ability to shape their own destinies was shrinking rapidly. GOBI-FFF resonated with these influential agenda setters and often money would be withheld if a country did not 'come to the table'.

Later UNICEF proposed more humane macro-economic measures calling for 'Adjustment with a Human Face'. It recommended, inter alia, debt rescheduling and guaranteed social safety nets as part of the 'adjustment package'. Child survival programs were to be prioritized.

In 1987 UNICEF launched the Bamako Initiative, a selective PHC package promoting community-financing

iv Growth monitoring, Oral rehydration therapy for diarrhea, Breastfeeding, Immunization, Food supplements, Female education and Family planning.

mechanisms as a middle ground. It was adopted in many parts of Africa and hailed by UNICEF as a success. But contested by many, it was largely abandoned because of its inability to make a significant impact on child survival.

The health market place

In the late 1990s under the Washington Consensus (World Bank, IMF and the US) structural adjustment policies and the drive for greater market-driven health sector reforms intensified. Donor countries were also in support of increasing liberalization trends. The rationale was that government-run services were bloated and inefficient, and the private sector could do better.

Privatization took different forms, from ownership of health facilities to outsourced service delivery (everything from management, clinical care to catering). Health insurance schemes also flourished. Transnational corporations from the North were the main beneficiaries. These trends would move $38 billion to the private markets in South America alone.[13]

But studies show repeatedly that left to their own devices, privatization efforts are not necessarily efficient or equitable and evidence associates better health outcomes with a larger role of the public health sector.[14] Cherry-picking the wealthier markets and skewing services to better-off urban areas, privatized health leaves the poor in the cold. Supposedly allowing for greater consumer choice, an increasingly fragmented health sector with a chaotic mix of private and public options, assumes a greater degree of health literacy than even educated consumers have. The cost of private care also makes a mockery of 'consumer choice' (although where public services collapse, private service use increases). Far from supporting the public sector, an unregulated private sector erodes it. It dumps poorer, sicker patients and the chronically ill on public services, undermining cross-subsidization and risk-pooling. It siphons off skilled personnel and large sums of money flow away from service provision towards administration and investor return.[15] In most cases, a downsized state is in no position to provide the necessary stewardship to regulate the private sector in the interests of public health.

The Bank devised a package of 'best buy' health interventions for low- and middle-income countries based on a 'cost-effectiveness analysis'. This has been widely criticized as priority-setting based on price rather than on 'need' or 'rights'. Two-tiered health systems evolved – one for the rich who could buy choice, and a Cinderella version for the poor, who would be forced to accept the Bank's package. Co-payments under 'best buy' plans meant patients also had to pay for vaccines and other preventive measures. Many just could not – with disastrous consequences including the re-emergence of epidemics such as dengue fever and typhus in Latin America. User-fees, instituted ostensibly to contribute resources so government could expand coverage, improve the quality of the health services and thereby improve equity, had the reverse effect.

Certainly, reforms to the health sector *were* necessary to achieve equity and many public health practitioners grappled with ways to achieve this. These attempts were very different from the market-driven efforts. The net effect of market-driven reforms was to reduce health from an inalienable human right to a commodity to be bought and sold on the open market. These were international trends in an increasingly privatizing world. Market-driven health sector reform has also eroded hard-won gains in the traditionally welfare states of Europe where solidarity values such as community risk-pooling and publicly accountable services are being dismantled.[16]

Other essential services such as education and water provision were also opened up to investment from transnational corporations and user-fees were also widely instituted. Here too there is no evidence that as a rule the private sector is better able to deliver. There are instances of public sector effectiveness and efficiency and there is evidence of failure and corruption on both sides.[17] Senior executives of Suez and Vivendi (two of the largest private water transnationals) have been sentenced in France for paying bribes to obtain water contracts.[18] Methods to ensure payments such as self-disconnecting prepaid water meters, banned as a health threat in Britain, are now on the rise across Latin America, Asia and the Philippines. They have been linked to recent cholera outbreaks in South Africa. Those who can't pay must do without, with all the knock-on effects on health. Remember Citizen Y.

The World Bank invested heavily itself in market-style health reforms. Between 1983 and 1999, the share of total sales of the Top 200 companies made up by service sector corporations increased from 33.8 per cent to 46.7 per cent in large part due to this trend.[19]

'Esap's' tales

SAPs exacerbated the debt crisis which spiraled by 400 per cent, reaching a staggering $3,000 billion by the late 1990s. Nigeria for example borrowed $5 billion in 1986, paid back $16 billion but absurdly now owes $32 billion. Across Africa, where one in every two children of primary school age is not in school, governments transfer four times more to Northern creditors in debt repayments than they spend on the health and education of their citizens.[20]

Even Argentina, which followed prescriptions to the T, and appeared to be doing well in the process, experienced a total meltdown in 2001 when 'conditions sparked off massive social unrest and the country defaulted on $155 billion of its foreign debt'.[21]

It is difficult to separate the effects of SAPs on health from the economic recessions that preceded their imposition. But in the 1980s, during the period when SAPs intensified, there are clear relationships between slowing of gains in IMRs and increasing debt[22] as well as other negative health impacts. In Zambia for example the proportion of hospital deaths related to malnutrition, from 1980 to 1984, increased two-fold in children under 5.

In the instances when SAPs led to growth, wealth accrued to an élite and in most instances did not lead to social development. Despite the fact that total world income increased by an average of 2.5 per cent annually, the number of people living in poverty increased by almost 100 million.[23] Inequities in the 1990s reached unprecedented proportions. The rising dominance of neo-liberalism – the ideology behind SAPs – with its deregulated, free-market economy, is in large part responsible.

Laissez-faire economic liberalization creates unrestrained market forces with potentially devastating effects. When the IMF imposed rapid liberalization in the former Soviet Union, élites got lucky but 10 to 20 million people died and almost every country in the former bloc experienced significant drops in life expectancy.[24]

Stiglitz maintains that 'inside the IMF it was simply assumed that whatever suffering occurred was a necessary part of the pain countries had to experience on the way to becoming a successful market economy, and that their measures would in fact, reduce the pain the countries would have to face in the long run'.[25] Yet after a plethora of UN treaties and commitments the dream of 'Health for All by the Year 2000' remains a dream and for multitudes the 'pain' continues.

The new targets on the block are the Millennium Development Goals (MDG) to be achieved by 2015 (see Chapter 7). While some progress has been made, it is clear that most of the goals will not be met on a global scale. So the goalposts will shift yet again.

No 'Health for All' by the 21st century

In the final analysis, SAPs, with their push to liberalize markets, formed part of an ongoing international drive on behalf of the North to facilitate transnational investment. Presided over today by the World Trade Organization (WTO) the last decades of the 20th century became the era of globalization where corporations run the global show and governments and international financial institutions often simply front on their behalf. The story of the effects of this on health unfolds in the next chapters.

1 J Stiglitz, *Globalization and Its Discontents* (Penguin Books 2002). **2** 'Progress for Children: A Report Card on Water and Sanitation', UNICEF, 2006. www.unicef.org **3** 'Making Every Mother and Child Count', *World Health Report 2005*, WHO www.who.int **4** 'Priorities in Health', World Bank, 2006 www.worldbank.org **5** R Beaglehole, R Bonita, *Public Health at the Crossroads: Achievements and Prospects* (Cambridge University Press 2004). **6** SB Halstead, JA Walsh, KS Warren, *Good health at low cost*, Conference report. New York: Rockefeller Foundation; 1985, in 'Public Health Innovation and Intellectual Property Rights', WHO, April 2006 www.who.int **7** T Evans, *The Equity Gauge.* **8** *The Ecologist,* Vol 29, No 3, May/June 1999, in W Ellwood, *The No-Nonsense Guide to Globalization* (New Internationalist/Verso 2001). **9** J Cliff, et al, 'Mozambique Health Holding the Line', *Review of African Political Economy* Vol 13 No 36, 1986. **10** JJ Hall, R Taylor, 'Health For All Beyond 2000: the Demise of the Alma-Ata Declaration and Primary Health Care in Developing Countries', *MJA* 2003 178 (1):17-20. **11** R Labonte et al, *Fatal Indifference – The G8, Africa and Global Health* (UCT Press, 2004). **12** D Tsikata, Third World Network, www.twnside.org.sg/title/adjus-cn.htm **13** 'Debt Relief and the HIV/AIDS Crisis in Africa: Does the HIPC Initiative Go Far Enough?' *Oxfam Briefing Paper* No 25, June 2002. **14** *Global Health Watch: 2005-2006* (Zed Books 2005). **15** M Fort, A Mercer, O Gish, (eds) *Sickness and Wealth: the Corporate Assault on Global Health* (South End Press, 2004). **16** Pollock, Shaoul, 'How the WTO is Shaping Domestic Policies in Health Care', *The Lancet,* Vol 354, Nov 1999. **17** Global Health Watch op.cit. **18** *Water Justice For All: Global and Local Resistance to the Control and Commodificaton of Water.* Friends of the Earth International, Amsterdam, 2003, in *Global Health Watch* op cit. **19** Research Institute Releases Study on Corporate Power on 1st Anniversary of Seattle Protests. Institute for Policy Studies. 2000. **20** W Ellwood, op. cit. **21** S Gloyd, 'Sapping the Poor', in M Fort, op. cit. **22** S Gloyd, op. cit. **23** World Bank, *Global Economic Prospects and the Developing Countries 2000* (World Bank 2000), in J Stiglitz, op. cit. **24** R Conquest, *The Great Purge: A Reassessment* (Oxford University Press 1990), in M Fort, op. cit. **25** J Stiglitz, op. cit.

2 Globalization: the slings and arrows of outrageous fortune

'It is important to recall that with our comfort comes a loss of innocence, since we profit from a social and economic order that promises a body count.'[1]

Paul Farmer,
Professor of Medical Anthropology, Harvard Medical School, and Co-founder of Partners in Health.

While the pros and cons of modern globalization are debated, one thing is clear: inequity has skyrocketed. Structural adjustment paved the way and international trade agreements are taking it to scale. With liberalizing markets, almost everything is up for grabs. Universal access to public goods is under threat, our genes have price-tags and you can die for lack of affordable medicines. Trade agreements are compromising public health policy.

MORE THAN ANY other time in history, the world is divided into those who have – often obscene amounts of wealth – and those who have not. Most of the wealth is in the hands of a few. Of the world's 100 largest economic entities, 51 are corporations and 49 are countries. The richest 10 per cent of people own 85 per cent of the world's assets. This is the era of globalization and it belongs to transnational corporations and their shareholders.

Globalization describes increased global integration in the 'economic, social, technological, cultural, political and ecological spheres'. For the haves, it defines a world more connected. The internet puts you in touch with distant loved ones at lightning speed. Our cultures are cosmopolitan hybrids – you can eat sushi in a Japanese restaurant in Johannesburg on a

Friday and slaughter a goat to your ancestors in your backyard on Saturday.[2] CNN beams out to every big city in the world. There probably isn't anyone on earth who doesn't know about Coke and the Marlboro man is one of the most recognized icons of all time.

There is an upside for public health. Through the internet and the ease of international travel, globalization has revolutionized the sharing of information and skills. It has facilitated an unprecedented cross-fertilization of ideas and technologies. Journals can be downloaded in seconds and Google will find you practically anything you need to know (unless you live in China where some sites are blocked). The internet has strengthened tobacco control collaborations and internet surveillance to detect disease outbreaks is a fine art. Human rights activists can organize global protests overnight. If the technology divide is bridged, Information and Communication Technologies could upscale distance learning and skills development to far-flung places. Clinics in remote regions can hook up to hubs of expertise for lifesaving advice.

But globalization has a dark side and many would say that from a health perspective, on balance, it is globalizing disaster. For starters, diseases can cross in airplanes from one corner of the world to another within hours. This is no joke in the context of Severe Acute Respiratory Syndrome (SARS) and potentially avian flu. International travel and widescale cross-border movements in this era certainly contributed to the globalization of the HIV pandemic.

But arguably the most catastrophic aspect of globalization is that in the neo-liberal macro-economic system that defines it, the right to health is trumped by the shareholder's right to maximize profit. It is characterized by global *economic* integration in which countries drop barriers to the free movement of capital, goods, skilled personnel and services. Protectionist domestic policies must go. Deregulation is the name of the game and with it, the minimalist state. It was ushered in through SAPs and continues to be facilitated today through conditions attached to debt relief and development assistance from the IMF/World Bank and Northern countries (see Chapter 7). It is entrenched through a growing basket of international trade agreements.

Proponents say the free market is the engine of growth and that growth will benefit everyone. But by all accounts, integration into the global free-market economy does not inevitably lead to growth. And economic growth does not inevitably lead to poverty reduction and development. While global percentages of poverty have decreased, absolute numbers have not. Between 1990 and 1998 the number of people living on less than $2 a day jumped from 2.7 to 2.8 billion[3] and inequities are larger today than any time in history. Percentage gains were largely due to poverty reduction in China (and to some extent India) which many argue pre-dated the full liberalization of their economies. But the free market comes with a price. Inequities are on the rise in both countries, already impacting on health. While some countries in the South may benefit, depending *inter alia* on the strength of their economies and infrastructure, most cannot compete with their wealthy counterparts. For them, globalization is a kind of colonialism on steroids, taking the 'global bargain-bin' phenomenon to new heights. When growth does occur, the impact on development depends critically on the extent of social investment in areas such as health, education and land reform.

The flip-side of globalization is socio-economic inequality, food insecurity, environmental damage and the globalization of harmful products like tobacco and processed foods. It is also the chaotic privatization of health and other essential services, the impact of which is described in the previous chapter.

There are strong associations between deteriorating

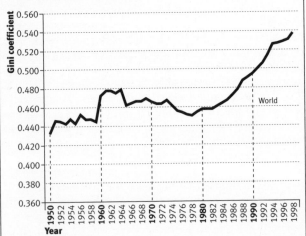

The Gini is out of the bottle

The Gini Coefficient is used as a measure of income inequality. While a few poorer countries are catching up with the rich world, the gaps between and within rich and poor countries as a whole, are on the up and up.

Gross Domestic Income per capita between nations (expressed in Gini points)

B Milanovic, *Worlds Apart: Measuring International and Global Inequality* (Princeton UP, 2005).

health and development indicators and the period of rapid globalization (1980 to 2000). Some studies have shown that in almost every measure in countries for which data is available, the progress achieved in the two decades of globalization has been considerably less than the progress in the pre-globalization period (1960 to 1980). There have been declines in GDP growth per capita. While life expectancy and child survival have improved, the rate of improvement has declined in all but the wealthiest 20 countries. [In some countries rates have stagnated and even reversed]. Public spending on education, school enrollment and literacy rates slowed in most of the poorest 40 per cent of countries.[4] So the question to ask is, 'why have rates of improvement not been maintained or even improved, if the invisible hand of the free-market ensures that everything will turn out well *for all*?'

The global trade fair

In the global market, international trade agreements set the rules of the game. They are developed in the corridors of the World Trade Organization (WTO) through its international pow-wows and 'trade negotiating rounds'. Rules are also increasingly set through Free Trade Agreements mushrooming between individual countries and regions. They are often even more pernicious than those of the WTO. Examples are the ASEAN (Association of South-East Asian Nations), and NAFTA (North American Free Trade Agreement) which binds the US, Canada and Mexico. The Free Trade Area of the Americas (FTAA), currently under negotiation will, if completed in its current form, bind the US and virtually every country in the Americas. Although punted as a door to growth and development, treaties like NAFTA have proven disastrous for workers in all countries involved.[5]

The WTO grew out of GATT (see Chapter 1) in 1994 at the conclusion of its 'Uruguay Round' of negotiations. WTO extended GATT's coverage from tariffs and trade in goods to include intellectual property and corporate investment rights, trade in food, agriculture and services. It also 'regulates' regulations for public health protections.

The WTO has 150 member countries, but is effectively controlled by the wealthier ones. Corporates in turn influence governments to act on their behalf often through significant donations to political parties and their election campaigns. They also dominate the various advisory committees of the WTO where all the real policy decisions happen. Their employees are at times paid by governments to actually represent them in negotiations. As a result, WTO trade agreements have been described as a 'bill of rights' for transnational corporations.[6] MTV's Bob Pittman once said: 'We don't influence 14-year-olds, we own them.'[7] Business could say the same about governments.

While treaty terminology implies consensus among equals, many countries have little say in the final 'agreements' and are not that happy with them. Many are bullied. Before the 2001 Doha Round of negotiations in Qatar, the US Trade Department informed the Haitian and Dominican Republic ambassadors to the WTO that refusal to agree to a particular proposal could jeopardize their aid packages.[8]

Whether global, bilateral or regional, trade fairs have similar ground rules. Once adopted, country members become bound by the agreements. If one country thinks another is transgressing an agreement it can bring a dispute against it. In the case of the WTO, disputes are adjudicated by a three-person tribunal which meets 'in secret' with no space for public scrutiny.

Regulatory chill

The playing fields are far from level. Getting entangled in disputes can be extremely costly and many countries lack the necessary expertise to engage effectively. To lose may be catastrophic. If Country A brings a dispute

---

Differential or indifferent?

Many WTO trade agreements allow for 'Special and Differential Treatment' (SDT) of member countries. This gives the South more latitude with compliance. Because people's survival is so inextricably linked to agriculture in parts of the South, many argue that at minimum, SDT should apply. Countries should be allowed to impose tariffs and retain subsidies where it will ensure development and food security. But most concessions relate to 'how long' a country can take to become 'compliant'. While richer countries are called upon to 'do their best' to take development needs into account, there is no obligation to do so. So most do not. The WTO's Doha Round of negotiations was meant to explore the implications of making SDTs 'mandatory' but nothing has come of this.

against Country B and wins, Country B must comply or face retaliatory sanctions in the form of penalty tariffs imposed on whatever area of trade Country A thinks will force B's hand.

Under some Free Trade Agreements (FTAs), corporations can sue governments directly. If successful, corporations must be compensated financially.

In 1997, for example, the Mexican state of San Luis Potosí attempted to stop the US Metalclad Corporation from installing a toxic waste site. Metalclad maintained that permits had been granted but agreed to apply for a municipal construction permit. Nevertheless, it proceeded to build. The Mexican state then designated the entire area an ecological zone. Metalclad declared a NAFTA dispute against the local government and won the case. The Mexican Government had to compensate the company to the tune of around $17 million.

With these stakes, countries often beat a quiet retreat when faced with a dispute, avoid situations which may lead to challenges, and back off from declaring disputes themselves. This phenomenon is called 'regulatory chill'.

There are meant to be exemptions, exclusions, limitations and preferences to protect health and developing economies. But they are often too subject to interpretation, too onerous to secure or inapplicable to the sectors that really count for development.

Globalizing harm

Trade rules are facilitating the global movement of tobacco, food and alcohol transnationals through opening markets, restricting regulation and encouraging mergers and acquisitions. These industries are contributing to the global escalation of non-communicable diseases including cardiovascular, respiratory disease and obesity. Globalization's contribution to the rise of these 'pandemics' in lower-

Globalization

and middle-income countries is discussed in detail in Chapter 6.

Ironically though, while the globalizing food industry is contributing to obesity through fast and processed foods, it is also contributing to undernutrition. While in Europe catwalk models may die from anorexia, malnutrition, according to WHO, is an underlying cause of 53 per cent of the 10.6 million annual deaths in children under 5. Malnourished children who survive may be severely compromised into the future.

Undernutrition has much to do with the free market. Transnational agribusiness (involving everything from farming, seed supply, agrichemicals, processing, marketing and retail) is bolstered by trade agreements. Controlling the entire food supply chain across the world, these transnationals have either co-opted local farmers to cultivate for them – opening them to the vagaries of the

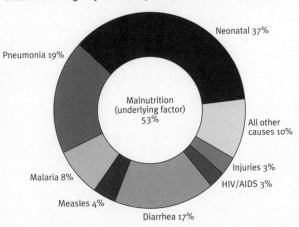

Dying too young

According to WHO, malnutrition is an underlying cause of 53 per cent of the 10.6 million annual deaths in children under 5. Malnourished children surviving may be severely compromised into the future.

Neonatal 37%
Pneumonia 19%
Malnutrition (underlying factor) 53%
All other causes 10%
Injuries 3%
HIV/AIDS 3%
Malaria 8%
Measles 4%
Diarrhea 17%

S Gloyd, 'Impact of Violence and Social Trauma on Global Rural Health'. Rural Wonca Health Conference, Sept 2006, Data from J Bryce, et al. 'WHO Estimates of the Causes of Death in Children', *The Lancet*, 2005 Mar 26-April; 365(9465):1147-52.

global market – or pushed them out. In both instances local crops are replaced with export ones.

As with SAPs, WTO's Agreement on Agriculture commits members to remove tariffs and subsidies for farmers and food exporters. But the current terms of trade remain grossly unfair. Through government subsidies for farmers in the North, the South has been flooded with cheaper food, making it impossible for local farmers to compete domestically and for countries to compete globally. A cow in Europe is subsidized by the taxpayer to the tune of $2.6 a day at a time when almost three billion people scrape by on less than that. Yet the South is expected to do away with its agricultural subsidies, remove trade barriers and open its markets. Some 70 per cent of people in the South make their living off the land. For this reason many argue that certain countries should be given special, preferential treatment.

Reaping what others sow
Indigenous farmers, usually women, have been 'genetically modifying' seeds over the years. They have devised natural ways to select seeds most likely to yield bountiful harvests. Their livelihoods depend on these seeds not just for their own crops, but because many farmers save, sell and exchange their seeds.

However, WTO agreements governing intellectual property rights allow agribusiness to patent plant genes. Thousands of patents have been granted on seeds and other genetically modified food-stuffs. Many of these patents are granted on the farmers' seeds. These farmers must now buy the seeds from the patent-holding corporation. Adding insult to injury, companies have developed seeds that do not regenerate, forcing farmers to buy again with each season. They must also buy the necessary herbicides for the seeds to survive.

There are some countries which have benefited from the globalized food industry with improvements in health and nutrition in young children. However, these benefits tend only to accrue when women control the household income (see Chapter 4).[9] But in the main, globalized food industry has contributed to food insecurity. It has devastated entire sectors of the agricultural economy, costing developing countries over $50 billion a year. All this is also less money to plough back into development. Agribusiness is also damaging the environment and through intensive irrigation may exacerbate water shortages.

The race to the bottom of the Bargain Bin

Liberalizing capital and trade markets has made it easier for transnational corporations to operate with impunity in other countries. They can literally go anywhere where conditions suit them, shopping around for cheaper labor and more natural resources, to maximize the return on their investments. When the Sandinistas in Nicaragua were voted back into power in 2006, business started packing bags. Coca-Cola marketer Karen Sandova said: 'We are just trying to figure out which country to go to'.[10]

Multinational corporations have moved entire operations into low wage/low tax countries with little environmental or labor protections. Export Processing Zones (EPZs) are the most extreme examples. In 2004, 5,000 EPZs employed around 50 million workers. China dominates but the Philippines and Indonesia are also big 'hosts'. The WTO estimates that between $200-250 billion worth of trade flows through these zones.[11]

Because transnationals can vanish to someplace else if workers get uppity, unions hold little sway and in some countries are totally outlawed. Countries bend over backwards to keep the transnationals, some using the military to crush labor unrest and waiving legal requirements on minimum wages. US basketball player Michael Jordan was paid $20 million for endorsing Nike trainers – more than the entire workforce was paid for making them.[12] Poverty and unemployment force job-seekers to accept unhealthy working conditions and pay – all a Dickensian disgrace. Beyond the scrutiny of unions and other watchdogs, companies get away with murder. Some 140,000 workers died in EPZs in China in 2003.[13] In Indonesia and Southern China working hours can be between 12-16 hours a day, 7 days a week. In Honduras, managers have reportedly injected workers with amphetamines to keep them on 48-hour marathon shifts to meet delivery deadlines.[14] Employees are predominantly women; many are on 28-day contracts, making it easy to fire them if they become pregnant.

Back at the ranch, with stronger labor laws and unions with more clout, companies in the North are downsizing their workforces and using casual contract labor. This absolves them from the costly social protection due to permanent employees and shields them against union demands. Again, women make up the majority of casual workers and so have been hardest hit. These trends have increased intra-country disparities. During the 1990s, the proportion of children living below the EU's poverty line increased threefold in Britain and today, about one in three live below this line.[15]

Hot money – currency is the 'new goods'

Health is also made vulnerable by capital market liberalization. Resulting in volatile capital flows of an unprecedented magnitude and speed, more than $1.5 trillion changes hands every day on global currency markets.[16] With around the clock trading, speculators are free to gamble on exchange rate movements, shifting billions of dollars in and out of countries overnight, often at the click of a mouse. When this phenomenon led to the Asian Tigers' collapse in the late 1990s more than 20 million people in Indonesia alone lost their jobs in one a year. Ethnic conflict flared under the strain. According to UNICEF 250,000 clinics closed and Infant Mortality Rates were estimated to have risen by 30 per cent.[17]

'Wither' national sovereignty?

Of increasing concern is the undermining, through trade agreements, of governments' autonomy to regulate in the public interest. For example, the Technical Barriers to Trade (TBT) agreement, the General Agreement on Trade in Services (GATS) and the Sanitary and PhytoSanitary Measures (SPS) are all agreements requiring a country's regulatory environment to be 'the least trade restrictive'. Legislation should not present 'unnecessary obstacles to international trade'. Together they influence the provision of public services, environmental protection and domestic safety regulation in many areas including foodstuffs, vaccines, medicines, diagnostics, blood products and other health-related technologies such as medical devices.

Under TBT, attempts by governments to keep out harmful foreign industries or to institute domestic health regulations to protect human, animal or plant life, health or the environment, could constitute an 'unfair barrier to trade'. The burden is on governments to prove their necessity and that there is not a less trade-restrictive option to achieve the same protection.

Because TBT and other agreements such as GATS eliminate barriers to the operation of foreign companies, they could prevent public health controls on marketing strategies for tobacco, alcohol, firearms and on the recruitment of health personnel. They could also outlaw pollution restrictions and occupational health and safety regulations.

Trade laws can also ride roughshod over international UN commitments. Guatemala discovered this in a WTO challenge brought by the US under pressure from the infant formula giant Gerber (see box: Who trumps WHO? on p 46).

SPS governs regulations that ensure food safety. It uses internationally 'accepted' standards to determine what health regulations are permissible. At face value this seems good. If I want to open up a business in your back yard, I should have to prove that it is safe. But SPS's purpose is really to ensure domestic regulation is not 'more trade restrictive' than required to achieve protection. Therein lies the rub. The international standards that serve as the WTO yardstick often provide for a ceiling on the level of protection. You can go less than the standard, but it is extremely difficult to go for gold.

WTO uses international food standards set out by

the Codex (Codex Alimentarius Commission). It was established as a joint FAO/WHO program but since it began to be used as the SPS standard it has become dominated by the food industry. Many of its standards are disputed. In 1999 for example, Codex approved a residue level of certain pesticides that were later banned by the US for use in fruits and vegetables because of their potential to harm children.[18]

If one country says its trade activities are safe, the burden is on the 'host' country to provide scientific evidence to the contrary (often a costly and sometimes impossible endeavor).[i] The EU for example has banned the use of potentially carcinogenic artificial growth hormones in beef. However, its attempt to prevent US and Canadian beef imports containing them was overturned by a WTO tribunal because Codex allowed for this[ii] and the EU was unable to provide evidence to the contrary. Considered a violation of both TBT and SPS, the WTO authorized the US and Canada to impose trade sanctions (equivalent to $116 million and Can$11 million respectively) on a smorgasbord of EU products such as mustard, cheese, pork and truffles.

The 'precautionary principle' – erring on the side of the safer bet – cannot apply when the jury is still out. Until all the evidence comes in, for instance, a country cannot stop a Genetic Modification (GM) company opening up shop within its borders. Think of this in the light of the early days of tobacco control, when the evidence of harm was growing but would not have been sufficient to convince the WTO.

Trade in services

GATS and FTAs facilitate transnational trade in services. GATS commits countries to successive negotiations

---

i Research is not conducted into many safety aspects in which case there may never be the required evidence.
ii Codex members were divided on the standard and it was passed with only a 'four vote' margin in favor.

progressively covering more service areas. Technically speaking, essential services such as healthcare are exempt but in practice, things are not so clear. There are enormous implications for universal access when service provision is driven by unfettered market forces. The impact of this on health services was described in the previous chapter.

There are now commercial opportunities for foreign trade in everything from clinics and hospitals, to health insurance, dental services, midwifery, laboratory and frail care. Where markets are not yet open, countries are supposedly allowed to choose what services they commit under GATS. Ostensibly governments can choose not to commit essential services. But countries are under enormous pressure to open up all services to international trade and with progressive realization in future rounds, it could really just be a matter of time.

In countries where service markets have already been established and opened up to competition, GATS locks-in existing privatization, effectively making it irreversible. In these instances exempting, regulating, reversing or extending public services into their domains becomes difficult. Its pro-competitive rules also create favorable conditions for further privatization.

Exemptions are conditional on an essential service being supplied 'neither on a commercial basis nor in competition with one or more service suppliers'. In reality, often due to SAPs and ongoing debt relief conditionalities, there is hardly one country that doesn't have some mix of public and private health services. Even public service user-fees could be seen as 'commercial'. In these instances, exemptions would not apply and countries could be open to a challenge. Thus SAPs has functioned as a critical precursor to GATS and further privatization.

Once health services are committed under GATS, pro-equity regulations such as capping the number of

Who trumps WHO?

In 1988, Guatemala passed a law in line with the WHO-UNICEF infant formula marketing code. The law prohibits companies from presenting their products as healthier than breastfeeding. With good reason. Thousands of children die every year because of diarrheal diseases related to infant formula use. Companies entice mothers with free samples which they give to their babies, but this means their breastmilk dries up. Then they are forced to buy formula. Formula gets diluted to last longer, compromising its nutritional value. In the absence of a safe water supply, bottles are hard to sterilize which often leads to life-threatening diarrhea. Knowing all this, in 1995 the US – influenced by transnational formula food giant Gerber – brought a dispute against Guatemala to the WTO. Flouting Guatemala's law, Gerber refused to remove its chubby baby face from its labels, or to add the words that 'Breastmilk is best' and indicate the age before which it is unhealthy to introduce other food into a baby's diet. Faced with a WTO dispute, Guatemala yielded and all imported baby food products were exempt from its law.

private health providers to contain costs, or regulating to ensure health services reach underserved areas would be a non-starter.

If a country commits a service under GATS, reversing privatization trends would be seen as denying market access. Similarly, expanding public services into areas previously serviced by the private sector would be seen as unfairly reducing the share of the market for foreign private providers. In both instances, if it proceeds despite a challenge, it could either face trade retaliation or be forced to increase liberalization of other sectors in exchange for withdrawing its GATS health commitments.

Under the investment rules of most bilateral FTAs, expanding a public service into areas served by foreign private providers would be deemed an *expropriation*. A successful challenge could require governments to financially compensate investors for lost business opportunities.

GATS has already liberalized health personnel labor 'markets' exacerbating the loss of skilled health professionals and contributing to the decline of health services in the South.

Services are lucrative areas for investment. According to public interest watchdog, Public Citizen, health care and education represent a combined $5.5 trillion market worldwide. Companies involved in water provision, for example, stand to generate $800 billion to $1 trillion a year.[19]

As with health, privatizing water provision has been disastrous in many parts of the world, including Latin America, Africa and Asia. Tariffs have priced water out of the reach of millions of poorer households with severe health consequences. Water privatization, full cost recovery and cessation of public subsidy programs for water remain conditions for IMF and World Bank loans.[20]

Even if a country had exempted its health, education or other essential services from GATS, many non-exempt service sectors covered by GATS have health impacts. These include services used directly by health care facilities such as data processing, cleaning, maintenance, catering, research, construction and waste disposal. Other areas with health impacts are insurance, banking, telecommunications, transportation, electricity, oil and gas production.

Forty-two countries have already committed hospital services to GATS, and even more to liberalizing services such as health insurance, dentistry, midwifery and paramedical personnel. But there are still huge untapped commercial opportunities in health and education particularly. While WTO GATS negotiations continue, the full force of its threat has yet to be realized by governments and citizens alike.

Trading in intellectual property

The Trade-Related Aspects of Intellectual Property Rights (TRIPS) agreement is probably the most infamous of the WTO agreements in the health arena because of its impact on health and scientific research and on the costs of lifesaving drugs. Shareholder rights to accumulate wealth hold sway over the right of millions to live healthily. Or even to live at all. TRIPS (and TRIPS-plus in regional and bilateral agreements) allow pharmaceutical companies to hold 20-year patents, preventing others from producing potentially cheaper generic drugs. The impact of these agreements is discussed further in Chapter 3.

So does wealth trickle?

If globalization is to reduce poverty through wealth creation and thereby improve health, the wealth must benefit all. But as outlined above, all the evidence to date says this does not happen within a *laissez-faire* set-up. Even free-market supremo Warren Buffet, recent philanthropist and one of the world's richest men, acknowledged on US TV that: 'a market system has not worked in terms of poor people'. Certainly, none of the big players are big on job creation. Between 1983 and 1999, for example, the rates of employment of the top 200 companies were dwarfed by their rates of profit. The sales of these companies make up 27.5 per cent of world economic activity but employ only 0.78 per cent of the world's workforce.[21]

Corporate tax evasion is a fine art. From the Bahamas to Bermuda tax havens allow investors to hide their money, depriving countries of important revenue to fund public services and social development. It is estimated that about $255 billion in tax revenues is lost annually because of this. The lifting of trade tariffs and the institutionalization of competitive tax regimes that come with a globalizing economy also remove major sources of revenue for countries in the South.[22] And speculative money cannot be tied up in 'development programs' because it needs to move whenever and wherever it wants. Hypocritically, industrialized countries grew their own economies through highly protectionist policies.

Is all lost?

So an unfettered global economic market does not seem compatible with public health objectives. But can it be better regulated to ensure development? And where is global governance, such as the UN, in all of this?

Many maintain the UN is not stepping up to the plate. WHO certainly holds little sway in the corridors of power. It has not been that willing or able to rein in the major drivers of market liberalization – the World Bank, IMF or its wealthier member states.

In 2005, 14 Southern countries led by Thailand and Bolivia put forward a draft WHO resolution to strengthen WHO's engagement with 'international trade and health'. The resolution also called on member states to include their health ministries in trade negotiations. However, Australia and other countries in the North managed to dilute the wording to such an extent that the member from Ecuador retorted: 'We need to be delicate in diplomacy, but we don't need to be so delicate that we end up being indelicate with our own people.' The resolution was deferred for everyone to have a 'rethink'.[23] Nevertheless the issue of trade and health has been put on WHO's agenda and a report by its secretariat acknowledges the links, including potential risks and opportunities.

But time is running out. WHO has already acknowledged that widely privatized health services make it difficult to respond to health emergencies. Pandemics are on the rise and many of these international trade agreements make it increasingly difficult to mount an appropriate response. One of the most dangerous could be the TRIPS agreement which is making vaccines, diagnostics and treatments unaffordable and placing at risk not just the people in the South, but every citizen on earth.

1 P Farmer, *Pathologies of Power: Health, Human Rights and the New War on the Poor* (University of California Press 2005). 2 Personal communication with

Globalization

Lebo Ramafoko. **3** World Bank, Global Economic Prospects and the Developing Countries 2000 (World Bank 2000), in J Stiglitz, *Globalization and Its Discontents* (Penguin 2002). **4** M Weisbrot, et al. *The Scorecard on Globalization 1980–2000: Twenty Years of Diminished Progress.* Centre for Economic and Policy Research; 2001, cited in R Labonte et al, *Fatal Indifference - The G8, Africa and Global Health* (UCT Press, 2004). **5** 'NAFTA at Seven', *EPI Briefing Paper*, April 2001, www.ratical.org/co-globalize/NAFTA@7/index.html   (accessed   31/03/2007). **6** R Mishra, 'Beyond the Nation State: Social Policy in an Age of Globalization', *Soc Policy Admin*, 1999; 32:481-500, in D Price, et al, 'How the World is Shaping Domestic Policies in Health Care', *The Lancet*, Vol 354, No 9193, 27 November 1999. **7** Interview with J Chilton Pearce, *Biophile Magazine*, Issue 6, May 2006. **8** N Hertz, *The Silent Takeover* (The Free Press 2001). **9** R Labonte, op.cit. **10** SAPA-AP, *The Star*, 7/11/2006. **11** M Finger, WTO, personal communication with N Klein, N Klein, *No Logo* (HarperCollins 2000). **12** T Lang, 'Public Health and Colonialism: a New or Old Problem?', *J Epidemiol Community Health,* 2001; 55: 162-163. **13** AFL-CIO (2004) *Section 301 Petition* [to Office of the US Trade Representative] *of American Federation of Labor and Congress of Industrial Organizations.* Washington, DC, AFL-CIO, in Global Health Watch, op. cit. **14** S Goldenberg, 'Colombo Stitch-Up' *Guardian,* 7 November 1997, in N Klein, op. cit. **15** M Dean, 'Absolute Effect of Relative Poverty', *Lancet* 1994;344:463, in R Beaglehole, R Bonita, *Public Health at the Crossroads: Achievements and Prospects* (Cambridge University Press 2004). **16** W Ellwood, *The No-Nonsense Guide to Globalization* (New Internationalist/Verso 2001). **17** Cited in W Ellwood, op. cit. **18** B Silverglade, 'The WTO Agreement on Sanitary and Phytosanitary Measures - Weakening Food Safety Regulation to Facilitate Trade', Center for Science in the Public Interest, 2000. www.cspinet.org/reports/codex/dutch_wto.html   (accessed   20/1/07). **19** E Shaffer, J Brenner, 'Trade and Health Care', in M Fort, A Mercer, O Gish, (eds) *Sickness and Wealth: the Corporate Assault on Global Health* (South End Press 2004). **20** R Labonte, op.cit. **21** S Anderson, J Cavanagh 'Top 200: The Rise of Corporate Global Power', Institute for Policy Studies, 2000. **22** R Labonte, op. cit. **23** Third World Network www.twnside.org

3 The politics of patents

'My children, some in high school and college by then, often sided with the critics [of the Pharmaceutical Industry]. They listened to my logic, but I could tell they weren't convinced, and to tell you the truth, I wasn't either.'[1]

Dr McKinnell, Pfizer Chair and CEO.

Technology has its role to play as one component of a comprehensive strategy to achieve 'Health for All'. But the benefits of scientific advances have not been evenly spread. The actions of civil society and a handful of governments have ensured that universal access to a sustainable supply of affordable vaccines, diagnostics and medicines is on the global agenda. These are entitlements guaranteed under international human rights law.

CLOSE YOUR EYES and imagine someone you love more than anything in the world. Now imagine that person is terminally ill. Now imagine there is a drug that can cure her. Now imagine that you cannot afford to buy that drug. Now imagine what you would be feeling about the pharmaceutical industry while watching her die. Would you be thinking that the high price is justified because the drug companies must recoup their research and development (R&D) costs which are a drop in their profit ocean? Would you be nodding your head in agreement when the CEO, who takes home $75 million annually and over $76 million in unexercised stock options,[i] says the prices are necessary to develop new drugs which will also help the poor? This, when you know most will only benefit the wealthy. Would you feel good that his company, together with the four other largest pharmaceutical companies, have a market

i Actual remuneration package of CA Heimbald, Jr, former chair and CEO of Bristol-Myers Squibb in 2001. (Families USA, 2001 www.familiesusa.org).

capitalization that surpasses that of the economy of India, and twice the GNP of sub-Saharan Africa?[2] Chances are, 'not'. Chances are, as you watched your loved one's intolerable suffering, you'd want to take up arms and storm the next shareholders' board meeting.

It was this kind of moral outrage that sparked the activism that shone the world's spotlight on Big Pharma.[ii] Antiretroviral drugs (ARVs) which have transformed HIV into a manageable, chronic condition in the North are priced out of the market for the South. Millions continue to die. Of the 6 million Africans who require ARVs, only about 11 per cent have access.[3] In contrast, 75 per cent of people in the North who need them, get them.

The world looked inwards and it wasn't pretty. Decent people felt ashamed and asked if this is what has become of our humanity.

While the focus has been largely on HIV/AIDS, the same applies to a range of other diseases affecting both the North and South. Vaccines, treatments or cures exist but are not universally affordable. They include drugs for communicable diseases such as pneumonias and hepatitis B as well as non-communicable diseases such as heart disease, high blood pressure and diabetes. Because the poor usually pay 'out-of-pocket' for medications, this situation is particularly unjust.[iii] It has been estimated that by 2015, over 10 million deaths per year could be averted by scaling up interventions for a range of preventable and treatable diseases that require access to essential medicines as part of their solution.

Yet in 2000 less than 10 per cent of global pharmaceutical sales went to developing countries. Latin America accounts for 6 per cent of this and sub-Saharan Africa, where the HIV pandemic is most

ii Big Pharma is the term used to describe the world's major pharmaceutical companies.
iii Costs are also debilitating for many people in the North, a large proportion of whom are not covered by health insurance.

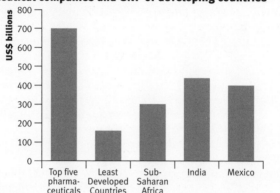

A bitter pill to swallow

Over the last three decades the pharmaceutical industry has ranked at or near the top in all three of *Fortune 500*'s measures of profitability.

Comparison between market capital of top five pharmaceutical companies and GNP of developing countries

severe, for no more than 1 per cent.

Access to affordable essential medicines was one of the 8 key pillars of the Alma Ata PHC strategy. Despite significant gains since its adoption, one-third of the world's population still does not have consistent access to these medicines. In the poorest parts of Asia and Africa, this figure rises to half.[4]

Under-budgeted, understaffed, weakened health systems, lack of political commitment from governments, lack of national investment and capacity for research, problems with distribution and dispensing, and corruption in the supply chain all play a role in this debacle. But a very big finger points in the direction of Big Pharma and at the root of it all is money.

Big Pharma makes a *lot* of money. According to Oxfam the industry made $400 billion in sales in 2002. The 10 largest US drug companies showed profits of almost $36 billion and their shareholders got a whopping 27.6 per cent return on their investments – more than 2.5 times the *Fortune* 500 average.[5]

To protect these staggering profits, the industry pays big money to ensure governments do their bidding. According to the Center for Public Integrity, the US pharmaceutical industry spent $182 million on federal lobbying between January 2005 and June 2006. Much of this influence plays out at the WTO negotiating table. The WTO's Agreement on Trade-related Aspects of Intellectual Property Rights (TRIPS) has been one of the big obstacles to affordable medicines. Completed in 1994, it requires member countries to pass laws requiring patents for any product filed after 1995. Patents provide protection for 'intellectual property' (IP)[iv] and are used to incentivize innovation in R&D. They prohibit a country from producing or importing generic drugs for at least 20 years. By preventing competition, drugs can be priced into the stratosphere. By 2005 all member countries had to align their laws to TRIPS. This deadline has been extended to 2016 for 30 'Least Developed Countries' (LDC).

While Big Pharma must tolerate generic production of its brands if they were developed before a country's patent law kicked in, newer drugs developed thereafter will be patented. This presents a particular problem for the treatment of diseases such as HIV, tuberculosis (TB) and malaria. This is because growing resistance to older, unpatented 'first-line' drugs and many patients' inability to tolerate some of them, necessitate 'second-line' options. With AIDS, where resistance is inevitable over time, there is already a need for third-line 'salvage' drugs. Yet these drugs will be subject to patents and will be priced out of the range of countries most in need.

As the world holds its collective breath on the verge of a human avian flu pandemic (WHO says it is not 'if' but 'when'), 20 years of patent protection is very scary

iv IP is defined as a product of the intellect that has commercial value.

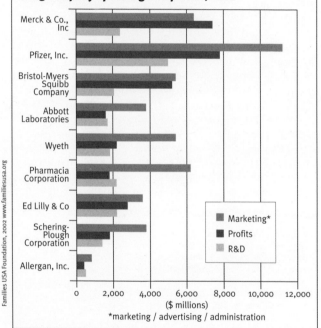

Big spenders

Drug companies claim that price reductions would force them to spend less on research and development (R&D). In fact the industry spends far less on R&D than on marketing, advertising and administration. There is plenty of fat to trim before R&D costs need to be cut.

Drug company spending and profits, 2001

Merck & Co., Inc

Pfizer, Inc.

Bristol-Myers Squibb Company

Abbott Laboratories

Wyeth

Pharmacia Corporation

Ed Lilly & Co

Schering-Plough Corporation

Allergan, Inc.

0   2,000   4,000   6,000   8,000   10,000   12,000
($ millions)
*marketing / advertising / administration

■ Marketing*
■ Profits
■ R&D

Families USA Foundation, 2002 www.familiesusa.org

for both the North and South. Similarly with 'Extreme Drug Resistant TB' – a version of the TB bacillus that has mutated over time to withstand most of the drugs that have been used to treat it. Spreading in many parts of the world and virtually untreatable, it is a powderkeg in the context of the AIDS pandemic.

But Big Pharma's argument goes thus: drug companies

invest large sums in R&D and patents help recoup these costs. Without patents they will not be able to develop drugs for the South. Without IP protection there is no incentive to innovate. Charging cheaper rates for the South will result in Northern consumers expecting similar or importing drugs from the South.

The counter-argument is this: substantial R&D for many drugs has been paid with public money through research institutes (such as the National Institutes of Health in the US) and universities. Additionally, research shows that Big Pharma inflates its R&D costs by around 80 per cent.[6] Whatever is spent pales in comparison to industry profits and to industry spending on marketing and remuneration packages. As to Big Pharma's last point, many countries in the North have laws preventing imports of patented drugs without patent-holder permission.

While the need to incentivize R&D is a fair argument, the use of the current patent reward system to do so is proving fundamentally unjust. So the most important counter-argument is a moral one – there is something

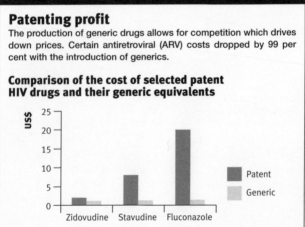

Patenting profit

The production of generic drugs allows for competition which drives down prices. Certain antiretroviral (ARV) costs dropped by 99 per cent with the introduction of generics.

Comparison of the cost of selected patent HIV drugs and their generic equivalents

C Pérez-Casas, 'Setting Objectives: Is There a Political Will?' HIV/AIDS Medicines Pricing Report Update, MSF, Dec 2000.

horribly wrong with a world in which people die because the medicines that can save them are too expensive.

Ironically, the US (one of the biggest proponents of TRIPS) expects Majority World countries to uphold patents regardless of the public interest, yet it had no problem threatening to break German-based Bayer's patent on ciprofloxican to protect US citizens against the 9/11 anthrax scare in 2001.

How flexible are TRIPS's 'flexibilities'?

TRIPS has flexibilities allowing countries to protect the public interest but the interpretation of these has been disputed. The WTO's Doha Declaration, coming out of the 'Doha Round' in 2001 made clear, after intense civil society pressure, that TRIPS provisions *do* permit country enforcement of public health safeguards to ensure access to affordable medicines. Flexibilities include parallel importing and compulsory licensing. Parallel importing is when patented drugs are bought without patent-holder permission from countries where they are legitimately sold cheaper. Compulsory licensing allows countries to issue licenses for the production of a generic version of a drug, even though still under

Bio-piracy

Big Pharma is happy to disrespect intellectual property [ownership] when it suits them. US company Pfizer almost got away with it in relation to hoodia, a local plant, before the San people in South Africa realized what was happening. For generations the San have chewed the hoodia plant on desert hunting trips. An appetite suppressant, it helped hunters go for longer periods without food and water. The CSIR, a public research institute, and UK-based Phytopharm patented the plant's key constituents. They sold the rights to Pfizer for $21 million to develop into diet pills for the North. The San people were never consulted and received no financial benefit until a Pfizer representative, challenged by journalists, maintained the San were extinct. A good lawyer and political pressure convinced CSIR and Phytopharm to compensate the San who will now get royalties for their traditional knowledge.

patent. Fair royalties are paid to patent holders. It also allows countries to import generics.

But very few countries have made use of these flexibilities. Firstly, procedures to issue compulsory licenses are onerous. Also, many countries lack the capacity to produce generic drugs and depend on imports. But TRIPS puts a ceiling on how much a generic-manufacturing country is allowed to export. This conundrum is known as the 'Paragraph 6 problem'. After much negotiation, a temporary waiver of the restrictions was agreed upon to allow countries greater latitude to export generics. Full of red tape, the waiver is also considered problematic. This certainly suited wealthy countries. More recently text for a permanent amendment was approved. Despite this, only five countries have signed up and so until the requisite two-thirds have done so, the temporary waiver applies.

But perhaps most of all, countries with vested interests in TRIPS have applied significant pressure on countries not to make use of the flexibilities. Those unable to risk litigation, trade disputes, loss of trade or aid, back off.

Meantime, corporate bullying is wide-spread. Charges of TRIPS violations are trumped up, and legal action threatened. Such is the case with Novartis, a Swiss company, which at time of publication was challenging India for refusing to patent Glivec, an anti-cancer drug for which it charges over $28,000 a year. Indian companies produce generic versions for $2,800. But Novartis is appealing against the ruling and challenging the constitutionality and TRIPS-compliancy of the relevant provision in the Indian Patents Act.

The basis of Novartis's claim is that Glivec is an 'innovative drug'. As India's patent law was instituted after 1995 it must allow patents for drugs developed thereafter. However, many drugs passed off as 'new' by Big Pharma are actually old drugs with slightly altered 'recipes'. The 'new' drugs have no additional therapeutic value. This process, called 'evergreening', effectively allows for the extension of patents. TRIPS, however, allows individual countries to determine their own criteria for patentability and to define what constitutes a new drug. According to India, Glivec is not a 'new drug'. If Novartis wins, India's ability to export generics and to deny patents for other non-innovative medicines will be under threat. This would be a disastrous scenario when about half the drugs used in the South are manufactured in India.

The scenario currently unfolding in Thailand is also indicative. Thailand wants to use Efavirenz, a Merck ARV, as a safer option for patients unable to tolerate nevirapine. Merck holds a patent for Efavirenz in Thailand. The Thai Government wants to issue a compulsory license for its generic production and TRIPS flexibilities allow this. If successful, it will cut the costs of Efavirenz by half. But the US Government is pressurizing Thailand not to embark on this course of action.

In the US, Section 301 of the Trade Act of 1974 requires the US Trade Representative to issue a yearly list of all the countries deemed non-compliant with expected levels of IP protection. Countries using TRIPS-compliant flexibilities often fall foul of this Act. The threat of trade sanctions under Section 301 is often enough to get countries to change laws even earlier than required under TRIPS.

The US reduced Argentina's 'Generalized System of Preferences'[v] program by half during a severe economic crisis, for failing to align its legislation with TRIPS – even though Argentina was well within deadline. The US also threatened the Dominican

v This is a formal system of exemption from the WTO rule which requires member countries to treat imports from all other member countries equally. The system allows wealthier countries to offer preferential tariffs to low-income countries.

Brazil's success with generic drugs

According to Oxfam, Brazil's treatment program – making use of generic drugs – averted 90,000 deaths and 358,000 AIDS-related hospitalizations between 1996-2002. The Government saved $2 billion.

Trend in annual rate of AIDS-related deaths, Brazil, 1983-2002

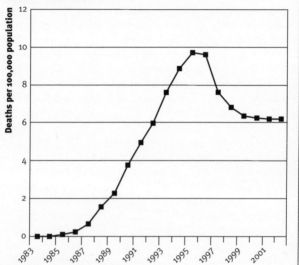

Ministerio Da Saude, Brazil. *Boletim Epidemiologico AIDS*, ANO XVII n1-1a52, 2003, in 'Public Health Innovation and Intellectual Property Rights', Report of the Commission on Intellectual Property Rights, Innovation and Public Health, WHO, April 2006.

Republic with trade sanctions for failing to comply with Big Pharma's demands.[7]

Annoyed with TRIPS flexibilities, the US in particular has been pushing through more onerous conditions (dubbed 'TRIPS-plus') as part of bilateral and regional free trade agreements (FTAs). Most countries have silently colluded. With the high stakes involved, resisting these pressures is not easy. In addition, according to Oxfam, bilateral trade agreements can provide access to the US market worth $11 trillion. Because of this, many countries believe it is worthwhile to cooperate.

The Hypocritical Oath

The industry's unethical marketing practices in pushing their patented drugs are also under the spotlight. Despite (among other incentives) 'free' meals and sponsored trips to overseas conferences, doctors still insist they are not influenced. Research shows otherwise. Some doctors collude knowingly. Many agree to author journal articles 'ghost'-written by industry people or get paid to do lecture tours conditional on them mentioning a particular drug a specified number of times.

Ethical lines have also been blurred by Big Pharma financing academic research. In the absence of legislation, getting full disclosure of data from clinical trials conducted by pharmaceutical companies, even to national regulatory bodies, is also a problem.

Neglected people, neglected diseases

Relying solely on market-driven R&D incentives to ensure access to technologies becomes particularly problematic when diseases only affect the poorer countries. With no hope of any lucrative market back home in the rich world, these are 'neglected diseases'. There is a whole Pandora's box of them including *Trypanosomiasis* (African Sleeping Sickness), Chagas disease and Dengue fever. HIV, Malaria and TB straddle the two worlds but because they predominately affect the South and hence are not a Big Pharma priority, they

Feeling low?

In December 2003 Britain's drug regulatory agency banned the use of Seroxat and other anti-depressant drugs for children because research shows they can cause suicidal tendencies. Investigations revealed that pharmaceutical industry clinical trials had identified this danger but did not disclose it to US or British regulators. In October 2003, the agency launched a criminal investigation into whether the manufacturer GlaxoSmithKline (GSK) had breached medicines regulations in this regard. No charges have yet been laid.

Source: S Boseley, *The Guardian* 10/12/2003 www.guardian.co.uk

are also referred to as 'neglected'. All exact an enormous
toll on people, health systems and economies. Chagas
alone costs $8 billion a year and WHO estimates that
Africa's GDP would be increased by $100 billion
annually if malaria was eliminated.[8]

For some, vaccines, treatments or cures already
exist. But because of the lack of lucrative markets,
pharmaceutical companies have stopped their
production. Take African Sleeping Sickness, for
example. A nasty disease caused by the tsetse fly, it
kills over 60,000 people a year. The methods used to
diagnose it are horrible and difficult to use in remote
settings. The drugs to treat it are toxic. Melarsoprol is
described as 'arsenic in antifreeze' and burns through
plastic. According to a Médecins Sans Frontières (MSF)
doctor in Uganda: 'It's a terrible drug. You don't feel
proud injecting it. It is caustic… and you don't know
if you are going to save your patient or kill him'.[9]
Melarsoprol kills 1 in 20 patients. Eflornithine, a safer
albeit imperfect alternative had been taken off the
market and only made available once an unrelated use
was found for it in the North.[10] There are no incentives
to find better alternatives.

New technologies are desperately needed for
this and many other diseases but Big Pharma is not
interested because they do not see profits. Technology
to eradicate TB, for example, is also in need of a
shake-up. The diagnostic tool cannot identify cases
reliably enough to halt early transmission. The only
vaccination we have provides weak protection for
children and is ineffective in adults. Current treatment
comprises a combination of drugs that must be taken
for 6 to 9 months. This is particularly difficult for the
people most at risk from the disease – poorer people
for whom health services are too costly or collapsing.
Often lacking fixed accommodation, they may also
find it difficult to have consistent contact with the
health system.

Relying on a market-driven incentive and reward system is in large part behind what is called the '90/10 gap' – less than 10 per cent of the world's health research money is directed towards diseases that affect more than 90 per cent of the world's population. In 2000, for example, there were apparently 7 new drugs in development for baldness but not one for TB.

Win-win or win-lose?

Largely in response to bad press, Big Pharma has upped its philanthropy. In the case of existing drugs, this consists mostly of one-off donations for patented drugs. Everyone agrees this is not a sustainable option. Unpredictable and contingent on goodwill, such 'bounty' makes long-term national health planning difficult. Big Pharma also discounts existing drugs but often this applies to one country only, for one specific disease – even if the drug has other applications. Pfizer, for example (and only after civil society protests) donated fluconazole to South Africa for use in one HIV-related condition. Only after further pressure did Pfizer extend this to other countries and for all other HIV-related infections for which it is registered.

And at the risk of seeming overly cynical, the donations and discounts are only possible because of enormous profit margins – the industry says it must 'do well' in order to 'do good'. Largesse also comes with great PR fanfare – and generous tax benefits. MSF maintains US taxpayers spend four times as much money to donate fluconozole to South Africa (through tax benefits to the company) than it would if it were to give the drugs through aid programs.[11]

Nevertheless, some companies have made significant long-term commitments. Merck and GSK are providing free drugs to treat river blindness and lymphatic filariasis respectively until the diseases are controlled or eliminated.

The pharmaceutical industry is also engaged in most of the Public-Private-Initiatives (PPIs), which are on the rise as a solution to the issue of 'universal access'. PPIs usually involve a mix of philanthropic foundations, industry (from food to pharmaceuticals), governments, UN agencies and the World Bank. Some are stimulating new research and aim to close the '90/10 Gap'. Others focus on ensuring access to existing drugs and technologies. As highly contentious entities on the health landscape, PPIs promise both risk and opportunity.

They have been welcomed by many as an innovative, 'win-win' solution to problems that are too big to be tackled by one sector alone. Some see Big Pharma's involvement as pragmatic. As one commentator observed: 'They own the ball. If you want to play, you must play with them'.[12] Certainly, some PPIs are delivering on their stated objectives. They have focused efforts. Millions have been immunized and ARV treatment has reached large numbers although much more work is to be done. There are drug R&D pipelines for neglected diseases. Millions stand to benefit if vaccines for malaria, diarrhea, HIV and other diseases are found. Billions of dollars have been disbursed.

But other people vehemently disagree with the 'win-win' proposition. Concerns range from entrenching donor-dependency to the risk of external agents determining national priorities. The sheer magnitude of philanthropic coffers, in the context of resource-strapped governments, is already skewing the public health agenda. Concerns are raised around conflicts of interest and accountability of key players. Many believe that private sector involvement in PPIs gives transnationals an inappropriate seat at the global public health agenda-setting table, providing another forum for the private sector to wield undue influence. Already under siege from powerful member countries, UN agencies' ability to advocate the regulation of the private sector in the interests of public health may well be further compromised.

UN role

Although UN agencies have increasingly embraced private sector partnerships, Carol Bellamy, former UNICEF Executive Director, did emphasize that: 'it is dangerous to assume that the goals of the private sector are somehow synonymous with those of the UN, because they most emphatically are not'.[13] By way of example, the president of the Medical Systems unit of US Becton Dickinson & Co. remarked: 'Of course we want to help eradicate neonatal tetanus, but we also want to stimulate the use of non-reusable injection devices, and to build relationships with ministries of health that might buy other products from us as their economies develop'.[14]

At the end of the day, corporates are required by law to account to their shareholders, not to the public good. So Big Pharma's involvement in PPIs often means more expensive (even if discounted) patented drugs are used. Certainly they bolster Big Pharma's public image, allowing companies to give with one hand while taking away with the other through the promotion of TRIPS and TRIPS-plus agreements.

Many people question PPIs' focus on single diseases

Who owns our DNA?

Intellectual property rights also extend to plant life and the human genome. Over 1,000 patents have been granted on human genes. This has proven highly controversial. US company Myriad Genetics for example has a patent on the BRCA2 gene that may predispose women carrying this gene to develop breast cancer. The company originally had a virtual monopoly on the diagnostics allowing it to charge exorbitant prices. Threats of a court challenge forced Myriad to limit the scope of the patent to Ashkenazi Jews, one of the populations in which the gene is more frequently found. There has been much protest against this decision but the status quo remains.

at the expense of other equally important ones. They also criticize the tendency of PPIs to rely largely on technological solutions, such as drugs and vaccines, neglecting health promotion and disease prevention. Existing solutions that would work if they were properly delivered are often neglected. As with vertical programs of old (see Chapter 1) their interventions tend to be poorly integrated into national health plans and divert resources from the strengthening of health systems (ironically essential to deliver these technologies) or the necessary socio-economic redress.

Without proper stewardship, accountability, and public interest safeguards including sound conflict of interest policy and public scrutiny, PPIs may solve some problems but perpetuate and exacerbate others. For this reason, there are calls for PPIs to be publicly evaluated and debated in order to map out solutions that address the concerns.

The Human Genome Project is often cited as an example of accountable collaboration. While people argue its ultimate benefits, it did bring together publicly and privately funded research institutes in the US, Britain, France, Germany and Japan, as well as philanthropic foundations, for the public good. For example, a core principle was that its research be placed in the public domain to the benefit of all.

What can be done?
The key to fair health care provision is to find mechanisms to incentivize R&D in a way that does not lead to gross price distortions. Some initiatives are attempting to share risks, costs and incentives between multiple stakeholders with shared stakes in IP rights.

There are already South-South and South-North partnerships conducting R&D into treatments for certain neglected diseases and many countries like Brazil, Egypt and India already have good R&D infrastructure. While innovation has happened in the

South (Cuba developed the first meningitis B vaccine) greater investment in R&D capacity is needed. The same is true for regulatory infrastructure, as is necessary worldwide. This will help ensure ethical research and speedy processing of quality drugs to accelerate access.

There are calls for an international mechanism to increase global coordination and sustainable funding of medical R&D, including for research institutions in the South. Ways proposed to stimulate R&D of new products include long-term procurement strategies with international and bulk purchasing funds, advance purchase commitments and guaranteed markets. Some of these solutions will also assist in negotiating better prices on existing drugs. Rewards and 'open source' approaches (similar to those of computer software) have been suggested as alternatives to patents. Sustainable funding should also be made available to non-profit product development ventures.

Addressing the fundamentals

In the final analysis, IP rights related to essential medicines and technologies should not be governed through the WTO and FTA forums that are driven by commercial concerns. Public health considerations must be prioritized and governance should be through public health institutions.[15]

Under pressure from Southern countries led by Brazil and Kenya, the World Health Assembly has given WHO a mandate to come up with alternatives to the current system by 2008. Scientists, academics, governments and civil society have put an alternative 'needs-driven' Global Medical R&D Treaty on the table. It suggests, among other things, flexible business models and IP rules as well as country obligations to commit budget to R&D support.[16]

While alternatives are explored, however, issues related to the existing system must be addressed. IP standards should not be uniformly high and countries should be allowed to make full use of TRIPS flexibilities. This means not pressurizing countries to introduce new patent laws before the stipulated deadline for compliance. Repealing Section 301 of US trade legislation would be a good start. A tiered, equitable pricing system has also been proposed with prices determined as part of an international and transparent system in conjunction with WHO. Countries would agree not to allow parallel importing of cheaper drugs to the North.

Involvement of health ministries in trade negotiations may help to ensure public health concerns are prioritized. Every effort must be made to ensure TRIPS and FTAs do not close the door on the generic supply pipeline. Generic-manufacturing countries particularly need to use the flexibilities and prevent national legislation enforcing TRIPS-plus rules.[17] Cutting the current red tape and extending TRIPS flexibilities needs to happen urgently. Oxfam recommends that patent-holders should have to prove their patents will not pose a threat to public health. UN agencies and the North should provide technical support to countries to assist them in making use of the flexibilities. Other suggestions include shortening patent durations and limiting their scope.

Solidarity between low- and middle-income countries to resist IP negotiations through FTAs is already happening. At the May 2006 World Health Assembly meeting, 10 South American health ministers issued a declaration on IP committing themselves to this. They also committed to intensify the use of TRIPS flexibilities and to 'ensure the supremacy of the public interest over commercial concerns'.

The courageous efforts of civil society organizations and some governments have put the issue of universal access to affordable technologies firmly on the world agenda. They have fought against huge odds – on the streets, in the boardrooms and in the courtrooms. They are a source of great hope that the current commercially-driven scenario will be replaced by a more just and equitable one.

1 H McKinnell, *A Call To Action* (McGraw-Hill, 2005). **2** *Human Development Report 2000*: FT500, 4 May 2000, in 'Cut the Costs: Patent Injustice: How World Trade Rules Threaten the Health of Poor People', Oxfam, 2001. **3** WHO/UNAIDS/Global Fund/US Government Joint Media Release, 26 Jan 2005. www.unaids.org/en/media/press+release.asp, in E Cameron, J Berger, 'Patents and Public Health: Principle, Politics and Paradox', Academy Law Lecture, *Proceedings of the British Academy*. **4** Medicus Mundi Switzerland. www.sdc-health.ch/priorities_in_health/pro_poor_health_service/provision (accessed 5 Dec 2006). **5** 'Robbing the Poor to Pay the Rich? How the United States Keeps Medicines From the World's Poorest.' *Oxfam Briefing Paper,* No 56, Nov 2003. w-www.oxfam.org.uk/what_we_do/issues/health/bp56_medicines.htm. **6** *Rx R&D Myths: The Case Against The Drug Industry's R&D "Scare Card",* Public Citizen Congress Watch, 2001. www.citizen.org. **7** 'Cut the Cost: Patent Injustice: How World Trade Rules Threaten the Health of Poor People', Oxfam, 2001. **8** http/www.oneworldhealth/org/global/global_burden.php (accessed 24 Dec 06). **9** MSF Fact Sheet. May 2004. **10** P Trouiller, et al. 'Drug Development for Neglected Diseases: a Deficient Market and a Public-health Policy Failure. *Lancet,* 359:2188-2194. 2002, in *Global Health Watch: 2005-2006* (Zed 2005). **11** Interview with R Cohen in J Bakan, *The Corporation: the Pathological Pursuit of Profit and Power.* (Constable and Robinson 2005). **12** Lucas, personal communication, in K Buse, G Walt,'The WHO and Global Public-Private Health Partnerships: In Search of "Good" Global Health Governance.' In R Reich (ed) *Public-private partnerships for Public Health* (Harvard University Press 2002). **13** Quoted in Peter Utting, 'UN-Business Partnerships: Whose Agenda Counts?', UNRISD, December 2000, in S Amrith, Democracy, globalization and health: the African Dilemma', www.histecon.kings.com.ac.uk/docs/amrith_healthafrica.pdf **14** DH Deutsch, 'Unlikely Allies With the UN - For Big Companies, a Strategic Partnership Opens Doors in Developing Countries', *The New York Times,* 10/12/1999) in K Buse, op. cit. **15** *Global Health Watch,* op. cit. **16** www.cptech.org/workingdrafts/rndtreaty.html, in *Global Health Watch,* op. cit. **17** 'Patents vs Patients: Five Years After the Doha Declaration', *Oxfam Briefing Paper 95.* Nov 2006.

4 The politics of gender

'No country can boast of being free unless its women are free.'
Oliver Tambo, former president of the African
National Congress, South Africa.

**In ancient Greece hysteria was a female malady
ascribed to disturbances of the womb. In 15th-century
English law 'the rule of thumb' allowed a man to
beat his wife with a stick no thicker than this digit.
Throughout history, views of women as overemotional,
second-class citizens have cost them their health and
their lives. But women have also been a powerful
force for change and have secured gains for many of
their sisters today. But there is still a long way to go
before we can boast that the world is free.**

WHO ESTIMATES THAT in Africa 10,000 pregnant
women die every year from malaria. Caused by a
parasite that thrives in mosquitoes, a single bite can
transmit the disease to humans. Pregnant women are
particularly vulnerable as the placenta has a receptor
the parasite likes to attach to. The mosquitoes are most
active at night and mosquito bed-nets treated with
pesticides have been shown to result in fewer infections,
miscarriages, stillbirths and fewer cases of low-birth
weight babies. The catch is that where patriarchy
reigns supreme, if there is only one net you can be sure
the woman won't be sleeping under it.

This is but one example of the impact of gender on
health. The best laid plans can come to naught if gender
is not factored into the equation. Gender describes the
different roles society constructs for men and women.
It defines what attributes and behaviors society deems
'appropriate' for each. 'Sex' refers to biological/
physiological characteristics. So 'sex' is about breasts
and penises while gender is about women earning less

than men, doing more housework than men, sleeping or not sleeping under a lifesaving mosquito net.

Gender is also about machismo – notions of masculinity which dictate that men don't cry, are fags if they have sex with men, should sleep with many women and fight violently if the need arises. Gender constructs allow men to rule the roost, literally with an iron fist and to be the ones who sleep under the mosquito net.

This is a sober reminder that while women in some countries fight against glass ceilings at the workplace, in others they are not allowed to drive, choose their husbands, retain their clitoris into adulthood or even live, should their husband die before them. You don't have to be Emily Pankhurst to see that none of this – including the glass ceiling – is very good for women's health. But if patriarchy puts men at the top of the pile, gender constructs also come with a price tag for them. Proving one's manhood makes men more likely to smoke, drive recklessly, have risky sex, drink more alcohol, take more drugs, wield more weapons and fight more wars. Seeing the need for 'help' as a sign of vulnerability, many men delay getting health care, with altogether unhealthy consequences.

If one had to tally up the burden of disease with gender inequality at its roots, it would constitute a global catastrophe. But we don't do the sums that way, so the health impacts of gender are often hidden and 'development' solutions often miss the mark.

From risk exposure to access to information and services, gender plays out in virtually every disease under the sun. Blindness, TB, tobacco-related ones (see Chapter 6)… the list goes on. There are too many to unpack individually, but the following examples are illustrative.

Sight, soccer and sublimation
Globally, two-thirds of blindness occurs in women. This is partly because women tend to live longer than

Lewallen and Courtright, 'Gender and use of cataract surgical services in developing countries', unpublished paper, BC Centre for Epidemiologic & International Ophthalmology, Canada in 'Gender and Blindness', WHO Gender and Health, Jan 2002.

Blinded by gender

In many countries women have less access to cataract surgery. There are many reasons, including less access to household resources to pay for transport and costs of care. In addition, they have less time to seek care and where female literacy is low, women are less likely to know about the possibility of eye surgery. According to WHO, addressing these inequities would reduce cataract blindness by 12.5 per cent.

Cataract surgical coverage

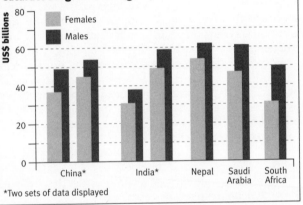

*Two sets of data displayed

men,[i] placing them at risk of age-related blindness such as macular degeneration and cataracts. But 'women's work' also places them at greater risk. Trachoma-related blindness for example is greater in women because their child-rearing responsibilities expose them to infection from their young charges.[1] Gender constructs also leave women less likely to access curative cataract surgery than men.

There are consequences for women's health in the most unlikely of places. Take soccer for example. While football fever in Germany soared in anticipation of the World Cup in 2006, so did fears that sex-trafficking

i Women tend to have higher life expectancies than men but their lives are more burdened with illness.

would escalate to accommodate the increased demand for sex-workers. As the fastest-growing criminal activity after arms and drug dealing, the sex industry nets around $7-9.5 billion a year. Two million girls between the ages of 5 and 15 are introduced into the sex market each year. They are forced into it through poverty, often lured with fake job offers and promises of a better life. Many are simply kidnapped while others are sold by desperately poor families or families that undervalue the girl-child. In this modern form of slavery, they face violence and rape and are vulnerable to sexually transmitted infections including HIV. Most are denied even basic health care.

Violence against women takes many forms from

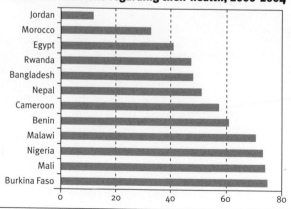

Men call the shots

Many women require their husband's permission to seek health care. In countries where certain forms of 'purdah' are practised, women may not be able to leave home, at least not unaccompanied by men. This makes it particularly difficult for women seeking help for reproductive and other confidential health concerns.

Percentage of women who say their husbands alone make the decisions regarding their health, 2000-2004

www.measureDHS.com

physical aggression to the structural violence of poverty. Whilst acknowledging the health ramifications of rape in general, the fact that much of it takes place at home is overlooked. Intimate partner violence often makes home the most dangerous place for women. Health impacts include injuries, depression and suicide, coerced abortions, pelvic inflammatory disease and infertility. Pregnancy seems to bring out the worst in abusive men and studies show high rates of associated violence, often directed at their partner's abdomen, leading to miscarriage, premature labor, stillbirth and maternal death.

Gender and HIV

In many countries gender inequity is a key driver of the HIV epidemic. Women are biologically vulnerable to HIV because the cervix is receptive and sperm sits longer in the vagina. But they are also made vulnerable

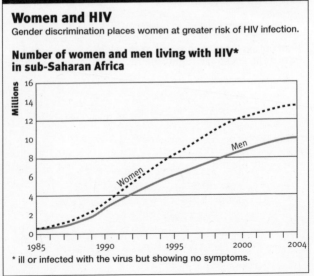

Women and HIV

Gender discrimination places women at greater risk of HIV infection.

Number of women and men living with HIV*
in sub-Saharan Africa

* ill or infected with the virus but showing no symptoms.

A Desclaux, et al. 'African Women Faced With the AIDS Epidemic', *Population & Societies*, No 428, INED, Nov 2006; UNAIDS.

because of gender constructs that reward men who treat women as conquests and that through privilege and control, deny women sexual autonomy. Under patriarchy, women lack choice and this is often compounded by violence. Studies show that women who experience intimate partner violence are more likely to be HIV-positive.[2] Violence against women places them at greater risk of traumatic sex which, with bleeding, increases the likelihood of HIV transmission. It also limits women's ability to control how and when sex happens. If burning a meal can lead, at minimum, to a clout, would you risk demanding faithfulness or insist on using a condom? Studies associate violent men with high-risk sexual behaviors. According to recent research partner violence may also push women into risky, often interconnected, sexual behaviors. These include alcohol abuse, multiple and concurrent partners and 'transactional' sex[3] – ie sex that ranges from relationships involving some form of economic benefit, to sex work. Underlying these behaviors are attempts to escape mental anguish, to assert some form of rebellion and to access resources that may, amongst other things, increase self-esteem.[4]

Poverty compounds women's lack of autonomy. Short-term survival and risky transactional sex for example with sugar-daddies or men with some means, may trump safer sex and long-term survival. Intergenerational sex, also often transactional, is a major risk factor in many countries where men even a few years older are more likely to be HIV-positive.

Beyond placing women at risk of infection, gender inequities often determine what happens to women who become HIV-positive. Imagine finding out at your antenatal pregnancy visit that you are HIV-positive (this is common). Would you share this information with a controlling partner? If you do and he blames you, you could be risking your life. You may be kicked, or kicked out of home. If you don't disclose, and he controls your movements, it may be hard to get care including medication to prevent transmission to your baby and to prolong your own life. If you are dependent on him financially you may never leave.

Gender determines the impact of HIV on women in other ways. As a woman, you may never have the female condom because it is costly and less widely available. You may never access life-saving health information. Someday, if current research is successful, you may be able to use microbicides. Inserted vaginally or rectally before sex, microbicides could provide protection from HIV transmission without your partner knowing. But because this research predominantly benefits women, it was neglected until health and reproductive rights activists exerted enormous pressure.

And when HIV leads to AIDS, the burden of caring for the sick affects women disproportionately.

One thing is for sure: HIV prevention, care and treatment interventions stand a greater chance of success if combined with approaches that address gender inequities at the roots.

Female Genital Mutilation/Cutting (FGM/FGC)

Globally, over 120 million women and girls are estimated to have undergone FGM/FGC and 2 million more undergo the procedure every year. FGM/FGC ranges from nicking, partial or total removal of the external genitalia – including the clitoris – to stitching closed the entire area (to be cut or forced open after marriage), leaving only a small hole for urination and menstruation.

Some argue that certain forms of cutting are part of an important rite of passage into 'womanhood'. As a pre-requisite in many societies for marriage, it is also seen as protective, providing economic and social security. Others see the practice as a means to subjugate and control, to ensure pre-marital virginity and post-marital fidelity (some women are re-stitched when husbands are away).

No-one can argue that FGM/FGC exacts an enormous toll on women's health. Impacts vary depending on the degree of cutting. At the time of the procedure many suffer intense pain and bleeding, both leading to shock. It can result in death. Other health problems range from infections, including of the urinary tract and pelvic inflammatory disease, damage to the urethra leading to incontinence, HIV transmission from shared instruments, menstrual problems, infertility, painful sexual intercourse, frigidity or lack of sexual fulfillment with subsequent psychological *sequelae*. Many women report that husbands have other sexual partners as a result, placing them at further risk of HIV and other Sexually Transmitted Infections.[5] Studies show that women who have undergone more extensive FGM/FGC are significantly more likely to have birth-related problems resulting in disability or death to both mother and child.[6]

There are many cultural and religious forces behind FGM/FGC and women who refuse it often risk ostracization, ineligibility for marriage and loss of childbearing opportunities. Today the practice is increasingly viewed as a human rights violation. The number of dissenting voices is growing and many women who have undergone the procedure are at the forefront of efforts to eradicate it.

Disastrous for women
In both human and natural disasters, women experience very particular health impacts.

There is increasing documentation of rape as a weapon of war, and increased gender-based violence experienced by women refugees in the growing number of humanitarian disasters such as floods and earthquakes. They may often give birth in unsafe conditions, even on the sides of roads. According to

The politics of gender

WHO, women suffered more spontaneous abortions after the 1984 Bhopal explosion in India, while in the 1998 floods in Bangladesh, urinary tract infections in girls increased from wearing damp menstrual rags which they could not hang out in public. Stories are told of families who, unable to hold on to more than one child in the floods, chose to save sons.[7] With massive movements of refugees where people are often excluded from public benefits such as social security and health care, women and girls are particularly vulnerable.

Poverty – structural violence against women

A staggering 70 per cent of the 1.2 billion people living in extreme poverty are women. There is not one country in the world where women have the same socio-economic and political opportunities as men and women score less on most indicators of socio-economic status as a result.[8]

SAPs and trade liberalization have deepened gender disparities. Under SAPs many women lost their livelihoods. Where trade openness has led to more employment for women, much of it is poorly paid, unhealthy work – for example in Export Processing Zones (see Chapter 2).

Women are generally paid 30-40 per cent less than men for the same kind of work, making it even harder for them to overcome poverty. And women often hold down two 'jobs' as the breadwinner and the primary caregiver.

They are often the first to go when jobs get cut and the least likely to be hired when jobs are scarce. Cuts in public and social spending have spelled more care work for women (tending to the casualties), and when the belt is tightened it is the girls who get taken out of school. The knock-on effect of women's education on household health has been well documented.

For poor women, who because of reproductive needs often require health services more often than men, the user-fees that come with SAPs and the ongoing privatization of health care have been particularly harmful. In some parts of Tanzania for example, utilization of antenatal care declined by 53.4 per cent in government hospitals after user-fees were introduced.[9]

In the South many women spend countless hours collecting firewood and water. This keeps girls out of school and women out of paid employment. In poorer countries women have less access to contraception, antenatal care and safe childbirth options leading to high levels of disability and death.

Parallel universes

A recent recipient of the French Government's fertility award told *Time* magazine that she is often asked if her nine pregnancies were 'wanted'. 'That always makes me laugh,' she said. '…do you really think it's still possible to have unwanted babies? That hardly exists anymore.' But elsewhere there are 80 million unplanned pregnancies annually and 120 million women who want to but cannot use contraceptives. They can't because they lack access to reproductive health services or because gender inequalities deny them the autonomy to make such choices for themselves. This is in part why in some Southern countries women face a 1 in 20 risk of dying from pregnancy-related complications, compared to 1 in 2,800 in the North.

Unmet need for effective contraceptives is particularly great in sub-Saharan Africa

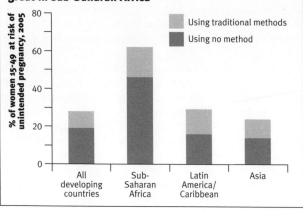

S Singh et al., 'Adding It Up: The Benefits of Investing in Sexual and Reproductive Health Care', New York: The Alan Guttmacher Institute, 2004.

The politics of gender

Poor women in wealthy countries suffer too. In the US, those below the poverty level are significantly less likely than women with higher income to have lifesaving mammograms to detect breast cancer. Black women in the US, more likely to be poor, are also more likely to be HIV-positive.

Today, 'Poverty Reduction Strategy Papers' (PRSP) must be developed for countries to be eligible for debt relief. They provide national planning frameworks for countries and are also increasingly tied to development aid. They are determining what resources get allocated where. But a major criticism of the PRSPs, amongst others (see Chapter 7) has been the absence of gender considerations in most of the country strategies.

From birth control to the right to orgasm

Yet despite gender's many impacts, women's health has been largely reduced to child-bearing issues. The first major 'maternal and child health' programs to emerge in Europe were at the turn of the last century, with the need for a reservoir of healthy children to provide a productive workforce and army. Women's needs were secondary to this imperative.

Political activists and worker movements in early 20th-century Europe began to promote women's right to health and by 1948, the Universal Declaration of Human Rights formally recognized the equal rights of men and women. This was the seed that would grow over time into a more radical human rights discourse for women. All subsequent declarations flow from these basic inalienable rights and freedoms. But if women's empowerment is defined as the ability of women to control their own destinies,[10] then despite the Universal Declaration, we still have far to go.

It has taken the world forever to reach a stage where international discourse on women's health has extended across her lifespan from birth to old age, and reproductively, to encompass everything from her right to autonomy and sexual pleasure. That means making sure a woman does not go blind from cataracts, as much as it means her right to choose who, when and whether to marry, and if, when and how to have children.

From the 1950s, mothers continued to be targeted as vulnerable but this remained a thinly-veiled concern for the child. It soon translated into vertical family planning programs, on the rise with international donors' agenda to rein in population growth. Women's health was reduced to 'birth control'. Contraceptive target-setting led to programs that were in some instances nothing short of coercive. Without consent, women were sterilized after birth or injected with contraceptives at clinic visits. In places, a deep distrust of public services resulted and what could have been an empowering tool for women, once again was used as a tool for oppression.

PHC vision
The vision of PHC articulated in the Alma Ata Declaration in 1978 provided initial hope for services that would address women's health more comprehensively. Hot on the heels of Alma Ata came The Convention on the Elimination of all Forms of Discrimination Against Women (CEDAW). CEDAW came into force in 1981 and is often described as the international bill of rights for women. Countries that have ratified or acceded to the Convention are legally bound to put its provisions into practice. It was a major milestone down a remarkable road of struggle for women's rights. Other important milestones taking place on the global stage included the 1985 Third World Conference on Women in Nairobi, Kenya and a decade later two watershed events – the 1994 UN International Conference on Population and Development in Cairo and in 1995, the Fourth World Conference on Women (FWCW) in Beijing, China.

By the end of the Beijing Conference, and building on

The politics of gender

past commitments, UN member states recognized that women's rights include the right to control and decide freely matters related to their sexuality. It confirmed women's rights to 'sexual and reproductive health, free of coercion, discrimination and violence'. The Consensus emerging from 'Beijing' was that women's reproductive rights were inseparable from women's socio-economic and political rights. It acknowledged once and for all that women's wellbeing is a right in and of itself and at

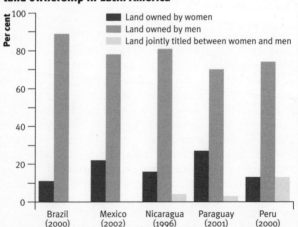

Land ownership can liberate

Lack of property ownership has been linked to poverty, HIV/AIDS, violence and other barriers to women's development. Ownership improves women's access to credit and economic opportunities, reduces dependence on men and results in greater decision-making autonomy including in seeking care for themselves and their children.

Significant male-female gaps in land ownership in Latin America

- Land owned by women
- Land owned by men
- Land jointly titled between women and men

Brazil (2000), Mexico (2002), Nicaragua (1996), Paraguay (2001), Peru (2000)

Note: No data were available for land jointly titled between women and men in Brazil and Mexico. Totals may not add up to 100 per cent due to rounding.

UN Millennium Project Task Force on Education and Gender Equality, Earthscan, London/Virginia, 2005, UNICEF the same time, is central to development. Its vision was for shared power and responsibility between women and men at home, at work, and in the wider national and international communities.

Beijing's 'Platform For Action' (PFA) translated these acknowledgements into time-bound targets. For example, countries committed to ensuring universal access to sexual and reproductive health services, to be delivered within the framework of PHC by 2015. In this vision, family planning would be integrated with all the services necessary to ensure women's reproductive health including screening and treatment for cervical cancer, HIV/AIDS and other sexually transmitted infections. The services would include the provision of antenatal care, and services to address gender-based violence. It also committed countries to development targets that would empower women and achieve gender equity.

Whose rights and freedoms?

The extension of 'reproductive rights' to encompass 'sexual rights' was a radical shift for the world. Interpreted to the max, it should encompass women's rights not only to control their own sexuality, but also the right to sexual pleasure. The battles waged to secure the wording in the final agreements are legendary. Activists and governments across the South and North formed alliances with one another as well as with international organizations. They were fiercely opposed by religious groups and conservative governments. At the heart of the opposition was the inability to swallow the right of women to make sexual and reproductive decisions independently of their partners and families.[11] Nevertheless, many couched their hostility in expressions of concern about 'Western' formulations of rights and freedoms and a lack of understanding of 'culture'. But the official African position put forward by the OAU (Organization of African Unity, now the

African Union/AU) puts paid to these objections. It approved the terminology of sexual rights and made the link between them and Africa's development goals, particularly through their impact on HIV/AIDS and violence against women.

Dr Nafis Sadik, former Executive Director of the UN's population agency UNFPA said, powerfully, that on all matters of culture and gender: 'We must be courageous in speaking out on the issues that concern us: we must not bend under the weight of spurious arguments invoking culture or traditional values. No value worth the name supports the oppression and enslavement of women. The function of culture and tradition is to provide a framework for human well-being. If they are used against us, we will reject them, and move on. We will not allow ourselves to be silenced.'

In the end, because of these politics, the PFA is a negotiated settlement; by no means the first prize. Nevertheless, these conferences forever changed the international discourse from 'population control and family planning' to 'women's rights' and 'empowerment'. To this day, however, many governments still simply 'talk the talk'.

Notwithstanding the good stuff, Beijing has been criticized for allowing wishy-washy wording that could let governments off the hook. It has also been criticized for trying to engender rather than challenge the 'national or global distribution of wealth and power, or current rules of the game on debt, aid and trade'.[12]

Women's rights
Nevertheless, the highly vocal articulation of women's rights emerging from these international events has reverberated across continents and empowered women, most of whom have never set foot in China. A woman in a focus group conducted on gender violence in South Africa said: '...[a] woman should not be quiet about her abuse... I mean we are not supposed to be suffering

The 'double dividend'

Women's rights are fundamental in and of themselves and are good for women. But they also benefit development, bringing what UNICEF terms 'double dividends'. Women in political decision-making positions have been shown more than men to push legislation that advances women's and children's wellbeing. Educating women results in improved child survival rates and school attendance. Research shows that when resources are scarce, women prioritize the nutrition of family members more than men do. A study by the International Food Policy Research Institute showed that if men and women had equal influence in decision-making, there would be 13.4 million fewer undernourished children in South Asia.

Increased maternal education is associated with reduced child mortality

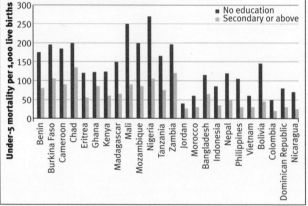

ORC Macro, 2007. MEASURE DHS STATcompiler. http://www.measuredhs.com, March 16 2007.

– we come from Beijing.' Sadly though, women's rights are seen as a threat to 'men's rights'. In a male focus group another sentiment was expressed: 'We are sick of Mandela's "50-50".[ii] Men are suffering. Women must stop their Beijing nonsense.'[13] Despite this backlash, many men are redefining masculinity and are rising up in support of women's rights.

These landmark agreements are a big foot in the

ii This refers to the emphasis on gender equality in South Africa's post-apartheid constitution.

door but the real challenge is to ensure their translation
into legislation and implementation at country level.
While implementation of the PFA by the 179 countries
that committed to it has been slow and even reversed,
there are many examples of significant progress. More
comprehensive sexual and reproductive health services
have been established in many countries. Countries
such as Egypt, Burkina Faso and Senegal have placed
bans on FGM/FGC and laws against domestic violence
have been enacted in many parts of the world. The
Global Health Watch publication credits Beijing
with initiatives in Brazil to ensure women's inclusion
in decision-making and property rights struggles for
women in Kenya. It is also credited with persuading
the Government of India to abandon 'family planning'
targets.

One step forward, two steps back
However, gains have been globally eroded by
the growing strength of right-wing and religious
fundamentalism and by the momentous parallel
changes in the macro-economic environment. With the
rise of neo-liberalism, beginning with the imposition of
SAPs and market-driven health sector reform, hopes for
comprehensive sexual and reproductive health services
have withered. The narrowed package of 'essential'
services to be supplied by an increasingly commodified
health sector gives little space for 'Beijing' targets.
Activists have lamented the lack of attention paid to
these macro-economic forces that snatched the carpet
from under their feet. Many acknowledge the need to
locate demands more strategically within this terrain.

The Millennium Development Goals (MDG)
discussed in Chapter 7 are seen as a further assault on
the gains of Beijing. As with all big international 'sign-
ons', they are a product of inter-nation bartering with
promises to 'rub your back if you rub mine'. Jacqueline
Sharpe, president of the Family Planning Association

of Trinidad, commented: 'Women's bodies still get to be the pawns in the chess game. They get traded away.'[14] However, the Millennium Project's Task Force on Child Health and Maternal Health, mandated by the UN to develop action plans to attain the MDGs, has proposed a greater alignment of the Goals with the Beijing vision.

There have been other developments since the MDGs such as 'The Protocol to the African Charter on Human and People's Rights on the Rights of Women in Africa' which came into force on 25 November 2005. With the blessing of the AU, the protocol reaffirms the need to protect and promote women's sexual and reproductive health. This, together with other policies such as the 'Abuja Declaration' and the 'Continental Sexual and Reproductive Health Policy Framework', commit African states to address the healthcare needs of all citizens, but in particular, the 'rights of women and girls.'[15] We will have to watch this space because there are already concerns that many of these commitments are not forthcoming. Well over half a century since the UN Declaration recognized women's rights as human rights, and despite the huge gains in many parts of the world, too many women are still unable to enjoy their basic freedoms.

1 P Courtright, BC Centre for Epidemiology & International Ophthalmology, Vancouver, Canada. In 'Gender and Blindness', WHO Gender and Health, Jan 2002. 2 R Jewkes et al, 'Factors Associated With HIV Sero-status in Young Rural South African Women: Connections Between Intimate Partner Violence and HIV', International Journal of Epidemiology (in press). 3 R Jewkes op.cit. 4 This section owes much to input from R Jewkes, Director: Gender & Health Research Unit, MRC. 5 'A Systematic Review of the Health Complications of Female Genital Mutilation Including Sequelae in Childbirth', Department of Women's Health, Family and Community Health. WHO, Geneva, 2000. 6 'Female Genital Mutilation and Obstetric Outcome: WHO Collaborative Prospective Study in Six African Countries', The Lancet; Vol 367 June 3, 2006. 7 WHO, Gender and Health in Disasters, July 2002, www.who.int/gender/other_health/en/genderdisasters. pdf 8 R Beaglehole, R Bonita, Public Health at the Crossroads: Achievements and Prospects (Cambridge University Press 2004). 9 AK Hussein, PGM Mujinja, 'Impact of User Charges on Government Health Facilities in Tanzania. East African Medical Journal 1997;74(12):751-57, in P Nanda, Reproductive Health

The politics of gender

Matters 2002;10(20):127-134. **10** A Malhotra, et al, 'Measuring Women's Empowerment as a Variable in International Development', World Bank Gender and Development Group Background Paper, World Bank, 2002. www.icrw.org/docs/MeasuringEmpowerment_workingpaper_802.doc. **11** B Klugman op. cit. **12** C Barton, 'Women's Eye on the UN', WIDE Conference 2004, http://www.eurosur.org/wide/Structure/CBS4_UN_2.htm. **13** Soul City Institute for Health and Development Communication, 1996. **14** B Crossette, 'Reproductive Health and the MDG: The Missing Link', *Stud Fam Plann*, 2005 Mar;36(1):71-9 **15** AU and Reproductive Rights, *Pambazuka News* 270 www.pambazuka.org.

5 The emergence of old and new epidemics

'Many political borders serve as semi-permeable membranes, often open to diseases and yet closed to the free movement of cures.'

Paul Farmer,
Professor of Medical Anthropology, Harvard Medical School, and Co-founder of Partners in Health.

In the last few decades the world has seen an emergence of old and new infectious epidemics. Simultaneously, 'epidemics'[i] of non-communicable diseases are also on the rise. They are both following the fault lines of inequity which create fertile ground for them to flourish.

NOT SO LONG ago the earth was awash with pestilence. Millions died or were scarred and debilitated for life from pandemics like the Black Plague (or Black Death), TB, smallpox and measles. Around the mid-19th century these infections began to be tamed. The 1918-20 flu pandemic, which infected 1 billion people and killed an estimated 50 million, was the last at such scale in Western Europe. A new phase followed with people living longer and having fewer children. This phase is characterized by non-communicable and degenerative diseases (heart disease, strokes and cancers) – the flipside of longevity.

In public health parlance, this pattern is called the 'health transition'. It describes the three predictable eras that populations pass through towards 'modernization' – from pestilence and famine, to receding pandemics, to non-communicable diseases. Many holes have been punched in this 'classic' model. With growing

i Many refer to the rise of non-communicable diseases as epidemics because, although they aren't caused by infections, they affect massive numbers of people.

inequalities between and within countries, populations have one foot in the first/second era and another in the third. There are growing 'pandemics' of non-communicable diseases that are increasingly burdening poorer populations and countries (see Chapter 6). But another unexpected curved ball has been messing with the model. Since the late 1970s there has been a resurgence and redistribution of old adversaries such as TB and malaria, but also at least 30 newly described diseases including HIV and SARS. Others, like avian flu, are waiting in the wings. Some are calling this a fourth stage in the health transition.

What then is behind this turn of events, just when we thought we had the wherewithall to keep most epidemics at bay?

New releases, re-runs and sequels

Some of today's epidemics have been around forever. TB has been found in 4,500-year-old Egyptian mummies and has been simmering amongst the poor community ever since. Others, like the HIV pandemic, are indeed new.

HIV took the world by surprise. Crossing over from monkeys in the early 20th century, it crept up slowly to explode onto the world stage in the 1980s. It has spread across every continent to become the leading cause of death globally among women and men between 15 and 59 years[1] and *the* leading cause of death in developing countries. It is said to have caused the single greatest reversal of development in human history. According to UNAIDS, in 2005 40 million people were living with HIV, 2.8 million people died of the disease and another 4.1 million people became infected. Over 25 million people had already died. The disease is thought to have peaked in the late 1990s and is beginning to stabilize in some countries. However it continues to rage in parts of the South, particularly in sub-Saharan Africa. There are also emerging epidemics in Eastern Europe and

Central Asia with new infection rates estimated to be rising more than 50 per cent since 2004. HIV is also staging a comeback in countries (like Uganda and the US) where it was previously contained.

TB kills nearly 3 million people every year. It once swept across the globe but with raised living standards, it receded in the North. However, it re-emerged with a vengeance in the 1990s amongst more affluent people in the US and Europe – a direct result of HIV. HIV has awoken TB bacilli that have lain dormant in hosts for years and has made people living with HIV more vulnerable to new infections, through lowered immunity. A major effort largely contained TB in the North but it continues to explode in the South and

The HIV/AIDS Epidemic in Sub-Saharan Africa – Fact Sheet', (#7391-04), The Henry J. Kaiser Family Foundation, January 2007 www.kff.org

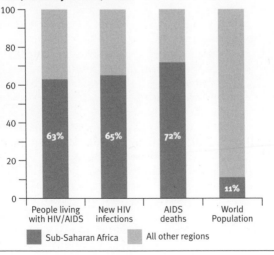

In the eye of the storm
HIV is the leading cause of death in Africa with sub-Saharan Africa at the epicenter of the pandemic.

Sub-Saharan Africa as a percentage of the global HIV/AIDS epidemic, 2006

	People living with HIV/AIDS	New HIV infections	AIDS deaths	World Population
Sub-Saharan Africa	63%	65%	72%	11%

Sub-Saharan Africa / All other regions

among poorer communities in Western countries with large inequities. China, Bangladesh, India and Pakistan, because of their large populations, account for almost half of the world's cases. Decades of neglect have led to the emergence of new strains of Multi-drug Resistant TB (MDR-TB) and more recently, Extreme Drug Resistant TB (XDR-TB) which is almost impossible to treat.

Malaria was also under control in most industrialized countries by the 1950s. In 1955, WHO launched a plan to eradicate malaria worldwide although the bar was dropped from 'eradicate' to 'control' in the 1970s. Some countries like India and Sri Lanka saw excellent results. Gains were also made in much of post-independence Africa with initial improvements in living standards and drug access. But from the 1980s malaria resurged – largely in sub-Saharan Africa but also in Asia and Latin America.[2] In the Abuja Declaration of 2000, all 53 African Heads of State pledged to halve malaria's impact by 2010. But, so far, not so good.

More recently the disease has begun to move into new territory.

What's going on?

There are multiple reasons for these sweeping epidemics. Over the years disease mutations and resistance to drugs and insecticides have developed. This happens regardless. But other forces are at play, aiding and abetting this process.

Firstly, as noted, the world is globalizing. Whilst in the Middle Ages diseases such as the Black Plague spread through trade ships, voyages also served as a form of quarantine. Sick people either died during long periods at sea or were no longer infectious by the time they landed. Nowadays, a person can travel round the world about six times during the most infectious stage of a disease. In our modern world, with unprecedented increases in international travel, this is cause for concern.

That's the glamorous travel. But there are also massive movements of people fleeing wars, displaced by natural disasters, or seeking economic opportunity in the face of grinding poverty. Over 100 million people move between countries every year, taking HIV and other microbes across porous borders. This has been a major engine of the HIV pandemic's spread.

Disease environments

In addition, a globalizing economy is drastically altering disease environments. In the case of malaria, deforestation of tropical forests for timber and large-scale export crops, together with mushrooming urbanization, have created more opportunities for human to meet mosquito. World Bank dam projects and commercial irrigation schemes have provided new homes for mosquitoes to breed in and also bring them closer to fresh batches of humans. Lack of prior exposure means people have no immunity and are extremely vulnerable.[3]

TRIPS and TRIPS-plus, the über-patent-protecting trade rules, are also in part responsible. There are vaccines, diagnostics and treatments for many of these epidemics that could save the lives of millions. But too often they are priced out of the market of the South. We have seen this with HIV where life-prolonging antiretroviral medicines (ARVs) have meant infection is no longer synonymous with death in the North.

With growing resistance to existing anti-malarial drugs, Big Pharma has also developed more effective ones. But these are priced for wealthier travelers and are unaffordable to the countries that need them most. With TB, lack of investment into more effective technologies has contributed (in part) to the rise of resistant strains. In the context of these twin epidemics, where TB is already the leading cause of death in HIV-positive individuals, XDR-TB is a grave public health threat. Malaria and HIV are also mutually reinforcing

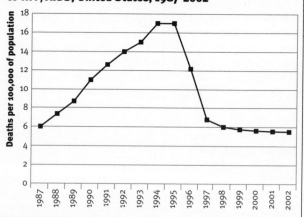

Money buys life

With the discovery of life-prolonging antiretroviral drugs (ARVs), HIV has been transformed into a manageable chronic disease with significant declines in death rates in wealthier countries such as the US.

Trends in annual age-adjusted rate of death attributable to HIV/AIDS, United States, 1987-2002

'Trends in annual age-adjusted rate of death due to HIV disease, USA, 1987–2002', Centers for Disease Control and Prevention, 2005, in 'Public Health Innovation and Intellectual Property Rights', Report of the Commission on Intellectual Property Rights, Innovation and Public Health, WHO April 2006.

and program interventions need to reflect this. HIV lowers immunity to other infections and can increase the severity of a co-existing malarial infection. Acute malarial infection in turn increases HIV multiplication increasing the viral load of HIV by about 10 times. This raises the risk of HIV transmission and will exacerbate existing infections. Co-infection in pregnancy increases the risk of neonatal complications and death. Because all three epidemics are largely associated with poverty, there are considerable geographic overlaps.

Running out of time

The next big thing could be an avian flu pandemic. Caused by the H5N1 influenza A virus, the disease has already crossed over to humans and in a few instances has jumped between them. Once this goes to scale we are in big trouble. Scientists say it is inevitable and international agencies and governments are already gearing up for it. Money is being pumped into vaccine development and there are drugs in the pipeline although still a way off. Although concerns have been raised around the safety of its use in children, Tamiflu appears to be the only viable option available at this time. But the world does not have enough of it and Britain has already started to stockpile it. Once again poor people will be the last in line. Even if the supplies are escalated, a 20-year TRIPS patent may literally be the death of us, as only wealthier countries and people will be able to afford it.

While things are more complex with HIV, by and large, as with most public health concerns, the rich are less at risk of exposure to most infections. And if they are infected richer individuals get a better shot at survival. Recent Harvard research shows that the influenza pandemic of 1918 (thought to be the great equalizer) actually hit poorer communities disproportionately. If the same pandemic were to occur today, researchers predict that about 96 per cent of deaths would be in the South.[4]

Fertile ground
Poverty and inequity create fertile ground for infection. Undernutrition compromises immunity, overcrowded conditions facilitate transmission, poor access to information and health services all exacerbate risk. Poverty and inequity also determine the disease outcome. Inequity in access to health services may jeopardize care and treatment. Poor service delivery leads to poor treatment compliance which feeds into drug resistance. Good nutrition is important to boost immune systems and medication may be less effective without it.

Socio-economic and political factors fanned the flames of the Black Plague of 1348. China, where it is believed to have originated, had just undergone a major civil war leading to famine and social dislocation. In Europe, the great famine of 1315-1322 – coupled with an economic depression – primed an entire continent to infection through weakened immunity. Added to this were the shocking living conditions, with poor people worst affected. This meant that populations did not stand a chance when the Plague reached Europe via the Silk Road trade routes. It killed about 75 million people worldwide. In a similar pattern, 19 nations were at war at the time of the 1918 influenza pandemic.[5]

Macro-economic policies dominating the world since the 1980s have deepened global inequities and hence vulnerability through large-scale undernutrition, lowered immunity and collapse of social services. In Eastern Europe and the former Soviet Union, IMF shock therapy with rapid privatization and capital market liberalization *sans* safety nets has caused poverty and unemployment with high levels of alcoholism and intravenous drug use. This has contributed in large part to the HIV epidemics which are now escalating in these areas.

Malaria is also re-emerging in the Soviet Union. It took 50 years to eradicate the epidemic there, but has taken only 5 years for the parasite to resurge.[6]

Many diseases, like TB, thrive in overcrowded living conditions, spreading rapidly as one person coughs close to another. WHO estimates that 95 per cent of all people with TB live in the Majority World. Cholera epidemics are also re-emerging in pockets as user-fees imposed on the very poor through the privatization of water provision and sanitation services mean that many live in unhealthy surroundings and go without safe or adequate quantities of water necessary for health.

HIV pandemic

The HIV pandemic is multifaceted with many 'co-factors' fueling it. A mix of sex, sexuality, stigma, and until recently, inevitable premature death, makes it extremely difficult to control. Where the epidemic is predominantly sexually spread, it involves ongoing maintenance of safer sexual behavior. Not easy to pull off, even for the 'fully empowered' who are more likely to be able to negotiate safer sex. Open talk about sex is essential but is taboo almost everywhere.

While there are strong connections with gross income inequality in many HIV epidemics, relative poverty (that is, having some means even though still poor by world standards) has been more recently identified as a factor, through its association with urban residence (more exposure to HIV), greater opportunities to travel and engage in transactional sex.[7] These associations certainly put wealthier populations at risk in the North. Strong urban-rural economic connections and good transport links in sub-Saharan Africa are also thought to be important factors in the regional spread of the epidemic. Economic migrancy, a feature of poverty and facilitated by these linkages, has been shown to be a marker of increased risk.

Gender inequities coupled with poverty place women at particular risk. This is discussed in greater detail in the previous chapter.

Recent studies point to the role of 'concurrent partnerships' in the epidemic in Africa south of the Sahara. These are relationships where one person has more than one regular partner, one or both of whom may in turn be involved sexually with someone else. Spread is rapid through these interconnected sexual networks because transmission is most likely when viral load is highest – in the first few weeks post-infection. In concurrent relationships one is likely to be having sex with someone else soon after infection. Complex factors underpin these relationships, but gender inequities, cultural constructs and poverty are part of the mix.

Epidemics in turn fuel poverty. HIV for example hits

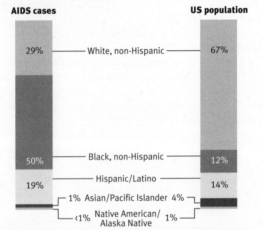

'The HIV/AIDS Epidemic in Sub-Saharan Africa – Fact Sheet', (#7391-04), The Henry J. Kaiser Family Foundation, January 2007, www.kff.org

All things are not equal

In a reflection of the prevailing socio-economic inequities, African-Americans are disproportionately affected by the HIV epidemic in the US. In 2003 African-American women accounted for 67 per cent of all new AIDS cases. African-Americans living with HIV have also been shown to have less access to medical care than white Americans and their survival time after diagnosis is less than other race/ethnic groups.

Estimated AIDS diagnoses & US population by race/ethnicity, 2005

AIDS cases   **US population**

29% — White, non-Hispanic — 67%

50% — Black, non-Hispanic — 12%

19% — Hispanic/Latino — 14%

1% Asian/Pacific Islander 4%

<1% Native American/ Alaska Native 1%

the most economically productive members of society. As a result, breadwinners become sick or die, farms lie fallow, food money gets spent on health care and children drop out of school. Poor households that absorb children who have lost parents to HIV become poorer. Many children are left to fend for themselves. With few social security safety nets, the poverty trap deepens.

As with most epidemics affecting the South, initially nobody paid enough attention to nipping HIV in the bud in these countries. Assisting the South only featured on the radar screen for the North when it became apparent that these epidemics could present a global security threat. The threat emanates from economic instability. When people compete for scarce resources, social conflict and even war tend to follow. Also, countries with militaries weakened through HIV infection in their ranks are also compromised in their ability to engage in both peacekeeping and in their own defense.

But by the time countries sat up and took notice much damage had already been done. Uganda's initial success was in part due to the strong political commitment at the highest level. But many governments across the globe continue to 'sleep on the job'.

Ailing health systems

A functional health system, with good primary health care, decent referral systems for more advanced treatment, caring health workers, adequate laboratory systems and drug supplies are essential to prevent and stem epidemics. Poor services lead to poor treatment compliance which leads to dangerous drug-resistance. Lack of attention to community involvement in treatment programs has also played a role. The collapse of health services in those parts of the world hardest hit by these epidemics is proving disastrous. The numbers getting sick are in turn over-burdening weak health systems.

In many Majority World countries, 'upstream' macro-economic policies promoting a minimalist state and rampant privatization have contributed to this. As discussed in Chapter 2, trade agreements such as GATS could further entrench inequalities of access. Many countries such as Botswana, Ethiopia and Zambia have dropped user-fees for HIV treatment but in those that have not, even a small fee presents a barrier.[8] Making poor people pay for vaccines and treatments is another recipe for disaster. This, together with decreased public sector spending increasingly bound to debt-reduction processes, is making it near impossible to manage these pandemics.

The emergence of old and new epidemics

Lack of commitment from corrupt, war-torn or weak governments has also led to under-funded health services. The drain of health personnel fueled by deteriorating conditions of service and globalized professional markets means there are too few to provide decent care. Tragically, many health workers themselves are succumbing to HIV, TB and other communicable diseases.

Fear of the 'other'

While epidemics may bring outpourings of love and support, they often reveal an ugly side of humanity. Fear fuels stigma and denial, pushes diseases underground and makes them more difficult to halt. In these respects we have not progressed much from the 14th century where Jews and lepers were massacred for 'causing' the Black Plague.

With HIV, gay men, 'foreigners', sex-workers and intravenous drug users have all been ostracized. Notions of divine retribution for sin makes people flagellate others and themselves. The stigma of HIV has led to frightening stories of discrimination, stymieing prevention and treatment efforts. Why go forward for testing or treatment if you risk getting shunned, disowned, and in instances even raped and killed if found to test positive?

Responses based on a human rights framework and the enactment of legislation to reflect this have been essential to addressing the HIV pandemic. Many emerging epidemics begin in marginalized groups. Countries denying the rights of communities most at risk do so at their own peril. According to UNAIDS, in West Africa where 95 per cent of people living with HIV are infected through paid sex, only 5 per cent of the national HIV/AIDS budget targets sex-workers. Many countries also deny the existence of men who have sex with men and so prevention programs neglect them. Stigma also dogs TB prevention and treatment efforts.

The earth is cooking

There are other forms of denial that are contributing to today's pandemics. Until recently, many people did not take climate change that seriously. Concerns for the environment were perceived to be largely the preserve of tree-hugging Westerners. Nowadays climate change has taken center stage with the realization that reckless industrialization has enormous implications for public health and the future of the planet. The delicate balance of earth's ecosystem that allows life to thrive has been upset. Massive burning of fossil fuels, deforestation and certain farming methods emit dangerous levels of greenhouse gases which trap the earth's heat, leading to global warming.

Experts say a 2°C/3.6°F increase in the earth's temperature is the tipping point for catastrophe. Since 1900, we are half way there. Over the next century temperatures stand to increase by 1.4°C to 5.8°C (2.5°F to over 10°F) – a rate without precedent in the last 10,000 years.

Global warming is melting the ice caps, raising sea levels, causing floods in some areas and droughts in others. It has brought extreme, unpredictable weather. WHO records a tripling of natural catastrophes in the last decade. In 2006, for example, over 160 countries experienced 354 natural disasters, affecting more than 100 million people. Beyond the injuries and fatalities these bring, climate change is causing a re-emergence of many dangerous epidemics. Epidemics are often the result of diseases borne by mosquitoes, ticks, fleas, bats and rats, which are sensitive to seasonal patterns. Mosquitoes for example thrive in warmer temperatures. They develop more quickly, multiply faster and suck more blood. It is estimated that with an increase of 2°C/3.6°F by 2050, 228 million more people will be at risk of malaria.[9]

As things escalate, it will not be like living in the Bahamas. With tropical weather spreading to higher latitudes, tropical diseases will follow. Diseases like malaria, bilharzia, Dengue fever, elephantiasis, river blindness, African Sleeping Sickness and yellow fever will increase. Some already have. The 1999 outbreak of West Nile Virus in New York killed 7 people and has since appeared in 44 American states. It is spreading northwards as regions like Canada start to heat up. In Italy, climate change has been linked to increased cases of visceral *leishmaniasis* (carried by sandflies) and tick-borne encephalitis. Italy was declared malaria-free in 1970s but this disease is also making a comeback. New areas of warmth will also nurture rodent-spread diseases including leptospirosis, Lyme disease and other infections.

Water-borne diseases such as cholera and typhoid will increase. A food poisoning bacteria, *Vibrio parahaemolyticus*, which is carried by shellfish and was previously confined to the Gulf states in the US, has occurred for the first time ever in warming waters off Alaska, Washington and New York.[10] The US is already experiencing outbreaks of *E Coli* bacteria and *Cryptosporidium* parasite following heavy rains. Both can cause severe diarrhea.

Extreme weather

Flooding and hurricanes (like Katrina) in heavily populated areas will displace millions of people into overcrowded areas where pests will proliferate and infectious diseases will spread. The 25 million environmental refugees of today will mushroom to 150 million by 2050.[11] The social epidemics that result from refugee emergencies, including violence against women, will thrive and increase vulnerability to infections such as HIV. Conflicts become more likely, as resources become scarcer. Floods and droughts will diminish agricultural output and food insecurity will increase vulnerability to infections.

Beyond bugs there will be other impacts. Surges in

heat-related deaths have already hit Europe. In industrialized nations, the heat-trapping accommodation of poorer citizens with no recourse to air-conditioning will prove deadly. Increased use of air-conditioning by those who have it will take its own toll on the environment with additional energy demands and use of the ozone-depleting chemical gas freon.

Globalized trade with market liberalization has allowed the industrialized North to spew out ever increasing amounts of greenhouse gases across the globe in pursuit of profit. Sir Nicholas Stern, former chief economist of the World Bank, and author of the British Government's report on climate change calls it: 'the greatest and widest market failure ever seen.' Former UN Secretary-General Kofi Annan warned that the effects of climate change could shrink the global economy by 20 per cent. It will affect everyone but as many point out, those least responsible for it will suffer most.

Can something be done?
In addressing the issues, economists say that cutting emissions now will cost less than dealing with future fallout. The 1997 Kyoto Protocol was meant to secure this. The biggest culprit (the US) has not ratified it, and neither has Australia. Critics believe its targets fall short of the necessary halving (some say two-thirds reduction) of all emissions by 2050. Its proposed Clean Development Mechanism could generate $100 billion for the South but risks commercializing air. It gives governments and private entities in the North credits for funding emission-reducing projects in the South. These credits allow the North to continue emitting 'back home' while still meeting their reduction targets. Similarly, carbon trading allows a low emitter to sell its credits to a high emitter so all turns out the same in the wash. The World Bank supports emission-

reduction projects while simultaneously investing heavily in fossil fuel.

Sustainable development – that which meets the needs of the present without compromising the ability of future generations to meet theirs – means we must all do things differently. We need to fly less and use more renewable power sources. We have to set better targets and redesign the trade rules to make the polluter pay.

Former British Prime Minister Tony Blair, at the 2007 World Economic Forum, called on US, China and Brazil to match Britain's 60 per cent reduction targets and asked the world to commit to more stringent cuts in a 'post-Kyoto' accord. Action that will make any real difference has to come at the highest government level.

Pandemics that once raged have been contained. We know what to do about malaria. There are already effective technologies (insecticides sprayed in houses and impregnated into mosquito nets) to prevent it. Diagnostic tests are simple and accurate and some treatments still work.

For a disease that exacts such an enormous toll, it seems bizarre that malaria is classified as 'neglected'. But it was not so neglected during the construction of the Panama Canal at the turn of the 19th century when US Congress paid generously to bring it under control so that workers could complete the task. Neither was it neglected when tapping into hydroelectric power potential led to its eradication around Tennessee. Comprehensive public health programs and raised living standards eradicated malaria from the United States. When disease threatens certain interests, resources are forthcoming. SARS for example, when it threatened the rich world, was under control in a relative jiffy.

Raising living standards has also contributed to the containment of TB. Through concerted efforts, HIV epidemics declined in Cambodia, Senegal, Kenya, North America, Europe, Thailand and Uganda.

Sustained efforts

Where epidemics are not yet generalized into the broader population, success with HIV seems to come to countries that focus their programs to reach those most at risk. Thailand reduced infections in part through legislating 100 per cent condom use in brothels. Non-compliance meant closure. Uganda's breathtaking early success (now reversing) seems to have been due to a combination of interventions including clear prevention messages, political commitment at the highest level, wide-scale social networking, sex education in schools and open public discourse on HIV. Together, this created an enabling environment for significant behavior change.

New studies showing that male circumcision appears to result in approximately 60-per-cent risk reduction in HIV transmission may make it the 'kindest cut of all'.

The resurgence of HIV in America, Europe and Uganda is thought to have come about because prevention programs were not sustained or failed to adapt as epidemics changed. Where emerging epidemics are percolating through marginalized communities of sex-workers, IV drug users and men who have sex with men, there is no place for being judgmental. Public health and social support must be swift and must protect the rights of those most vulnerable.

Reversing these pandemics has to be high up on the world agenda for years to come. More resources are being committed today than ever before. The US, albeit with problematic conditionalities, has donated over $15 billion to scaling up prevention and treatment in the worst-affected countries.

The Global Fund to Fight AIDS, TB and Malaria has channeled almost $3 billion to vulnerable areas, but funding the Fund remains far below target. The G8's Gleneagles commitment to donate $3.7 billion is already falling short. Yet according to consumer rights organization, Public Citizen, the annual amount spent by rich countries on aid for HIV amounts to just three days' spending on military hardware.

Public-Private-Initiatives (PPI), also not without controversy (see Chapter 3), have been set up to develop new drugs and explore vaccines and other technologies to address key epidemics.

Slow response

But while technological advances remain somewhat of a holy grail, we need to accelerate the interventions that we already know work. With HIV, upscaling prevention efforts along with affordable treatment, care and support for those living with HIV remains the mainstay of our efforts. Political commitment at the highest level is necessary to pull this all off and increased voice given to people who are HIV-positive.

Despite having existing solutions to these epidemics, the world has been sluggish in responding. Perhaps, as always, we will have to wait until epidemics turn up on the doorstep of the North. Perhaps global warming will be the phenomenon to do that, bringing a host of infections into contact with the more privileged.

That is probably why the world will pull out the stops to prevent an avian flu pandemic. A lot of money is already going into early detection and vaccine development. Vietnam has had considerable success in containing the epidemic in its bird population. Over 140 million birds have already been culled worldwide. Awareness is increasing and even the G8 has a flu pandemic alert on its agenda. Innovation is on the rise. We need to know the minute a chicken coughs. The Canadian Global Public Health Intelligence Network (GPHIN) has pioneered internet surveillance to detect early warnings of bird flu and other infectious outbreaks. It played a critical role in the response to SARS. Cellular/mobile phone technology in Rwanda is helping doctors track avian flu (as well as HIV).

But in the scale of things, our response has been mild.

Poultry farmers must be compensated and there is not enough of a piggy bank for this yet. On the health side, systems have to be in place to enable rapid diagnosis, even in far-flung villages. Health services need to be strengthened. Vaccines and cures are still a way off and early detection and rapid response are currently our best hopes.

The number-crunching predictions are already flying fast and furious – WHO warns that avian flu could make a billion sick, hospitalize 28 million and kill up to 7 million. We know that when SARS threatened the North it *did* pull out all the stops. Can we be sure the same will happen for countries in the South if and when avian flu strikes? The track record is not great. Policy-makers have however been meeting to discuss how the needs and interests of the most disadvantaged can be addressed in the global response. Time will tell.

Despite tragedy, some people point to progress that follows in the wake of pandemics. For example, the Renaissance explosion of innovation in the sciences can be linked to the Black Plague that preceded it. The 1918 flu pandemic is seen as a spur to advances in the practice of public health and the recognition of public health's central role in economic development and social stability.

Surveillance mechanisms set up for one pandemic can be used for another, and the development of new vaccines and treatments have spin-offs for other diseases. The HIV pandemic has led to social dislocation and discrimination, but also rallied people together and built social cohesion. This has other positive knock-on effects. Strengthening health systems will deliver multiple health benefits.

But above all, we must get to the roots. Countries that moved into the third stage of the health transition did so in large part because of raised living standards and better nutrition. Technologies that helped somewhat then, stand to make a huge difference today. But inequities interfere in access to all the above. Whether emerging or re-emerging, these epidemics lay bare what this book has stressed: that many illnesses follow the fault-lines of inequity and that people who are poor and dispossessed, including women, almost always suffer disproportionately.

This is increasingly the case with conditions such as diabetes, heart disease, strokes, and cancers which are globalizing exponentially. The next chapter looks at two of the industries largely responsible for the emergence of these non-communicable 'epidemics'.

1 A de Francisco, S Matlin, (eds) *Monitoring Financial Flows for Health Research 2006*, Global Forum for Health Research, 2006, www.globalforumhealth.org **2** T Holtz, SP Kachur, 'The Reglobalization of Malaria', in M Fort, MA Mercer, O Gish, (eds) *Sickness and Wealth: The Corporate Assault on Global Health* (South End Press, 2004). **3** T Holtz, op cit. **4** Cited in *Harvard Public Health Review*. Spring 2005. **5** Wikipedia **6** Cited in *The New Yorker*, 24/10/2005. **7** S Gillespie, R Greener, 'Is Poverty or Wealth Driving HIV Transmission?' Working paper for the UNAIDS Technical Consultation on Prevention of Sexual Transmission of HIV, Geneva, 19/9/2006. **8** 'Step Up the Pace of HIV Prevention in Africa'. *Fact sheet* www. afro.who.int/accelerate_hiv_prevention/fact_sheets.pdf. **9** *Global Health Watch: 2005-2006* (Zed Books Ltd, London, 2005). **10** Physicians for Social Responsibility www.psr.org/site/PageServer?pagename=enviro_resources (accessed 23 Dec 2006). **11** *Global Health Watch*, op. cit.

6 Non-communicable 'pandemics': the high price of Big Business

*'It would be stupid to ignore a growing market.
I can't answer the moral dilemma. We are in the
business of pleasing our shareholders.'*
    Manager at Rothmans Export Ltd on the ethics of
                marketing cigarettes to the South.[1]

**The rise of non-communicable diseases presents a
major challenge. Formerly described as 'diseases
of the aristocracy', these are now widespread in
low- and middle-income populations. This is mainly
because globalizing industries are searching out new
markets both at home and abroad. This chapter looks
at two culprits, the tobacco and food industries.**

SOME 35 MILLION people die every year from non-
communicable, chronic diseases. The big ones are
coronary heart disease, strokes, cancers, chronic lung
disease and diabetes. They are largely preventable
conditions and, without action, WHO estimates deaths
will increase by 17 per cent between 2005 and 2015 to
41 million.

Largely perceived as lifestyle diseases of the comfy
classes, they are increasingly affecting poor people.
Cardiovascular disease is the world's leading cause of
death with 80 per cent of its burden affecting low- and
middle-income countries. By 2010, India will have the
largest number of diabetics in the world.

The causes of these diseases are many. In some,
genetic factors play a role. Also, people are living
longer and many non-communicable diseases come
with age. Infections with Human Papilloma Virus and
Hepatitis B (both more common in poor communities)
are leading to increased rates of cervical and liver
cancers respectively in the countries of the South.

Non-communicable 'pandemics'

The 'double burden'

WHO estimates that 80 per cent of the 35 million annual deaths due to non-communicable diseases in 2005 occurred in low- and middle-income countries. In the South, non-communicable and communicable pandemics are mutually reinforcing. Some infectious agents cause cancers and smoking increases TB mortality. Dealing with chronic diseases will also contribute to a decline in infectious pandemics.

Mortality conditions by level of income, 2002 estimates

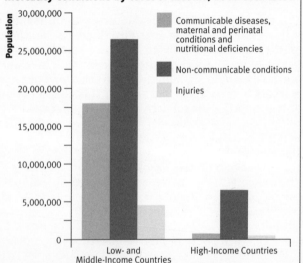

C Mathers, A de Francisco, *The Global Burden of Disease*, in MA Burke, A de Francisco (eds), *Monitoring Financial Flows for Health Research 2004*, Global Forum for Health Research, Geneva, 2004, Chapter 3, 53-67.

Many chronic diseases are linked to low birth weight and to urbanization (both associated with poverty). But most are underpinned by similar risk factors – obesity, tobacco, alcohol and inactivity. Because of this, those affected are often blamed – for gluttony, laziness, smoking and boozing. But much of the blame should be laid at the door of globalizing 'Western lifestyles' and powerful players such as the food, alcohol and tobacco industries. In addition, polluting industries cause asthma and lung disease. Collectively, these industries are creating what Yale nutrition and obesity expert Kelly Bronwell describes as a 'toxic' environment that hampers individuals' ability to make healthy choices.

Tobacco – a drug by any other name

The tobacco industry carries the name-tag of 'evil empire' – with good reason. How else can one describe an industry that continues to push its products knowing that they are lethal with no safe way to be consumed? Big Tobacco spent over $15.2 billion in 2003 on marketing and promotions in the US alone. And if this is not enough to convince one of the industry's iniquitous ways, how about if one knew (as is true) that industry devised ways to make cigarettes even more addictive and to increase the number of puffs per cigarette. Here is what Imperial Tobacco Ltd-Canada's market research was saying in 1982: 'The desire to quit seems to come earlier now than before, even prior to the end of high school. In fact it often seems to take hold as soon as the recent starter admits to himself that he is hooked on smoking. However the desire to quit, and actually carrying it out, are two quite different things, as the would-be quitter soon learns.'[2] Litigation unleashed an avalanche of similarly unsavory information from industry archives, showing it to be unscrupulous and deceptive; some would even say murderous.

Around 5 million people die prematurely from tobacco-related illness each year. It is the leading cause of adult deaths in the North and the fastest-growing cause of deaths worldwide.[3] For every cigarette you smoke, you lose 7 minutes of your life. The litany of illness associated with actively or passively smoking is huge – from lung cancer, emphysema and heart disease, to cervical cancer, infertility, premature menopause, miscarriage and low birth weight babies. Children with parents who smoke are more at risk of Sudden Infant Death Syndrome and everything from asthma to ear infections. According to WHO, about 250 million

Non-communicable 'pandemics'

of the 700 million children passively smoking will die from tobacco-related diseases. This is horrific, but is to be expected of a substance that contains over 43 known carcinogens.

According to WHO, the cost of health care due to tobacco-related ailments ranges from 0.1 to 1.1 per cent of GDP in high income countries. It costs India $8 billion in health care alone. In China a poor man may spend up to 60 per cent of his income on cigarettes. This means trade-offs with food or school money. It is estimated that in Bangladesh 10.5 million fewer people would be malnourished if smoking were to stop. Loss of family and breadwinner, absenteeism and funeral costs all exact a social and economic toll. In the Majority World, tobacco farming – with most of the profits going to industry – uses valuable land that could be used for food crops. Workers are badly paid and vulnerable to pesticide poisoning and Green Tobacco Sickness.[i] The high nutrient requirement of tobacco leads to soil degradation which is associated with pest infestation. This leads to heavy use of fertilizers. The intensive burning of wood in curing and processing the tobacco leaf results in large-scale deforestation and contributes to climate change. Large amounts of pesticides are needed for tobacco production and cause ground and water pollution.

Have we come a long way baby?
While control legislation and bad press have led to declines in tobacco consumption in the North, higher rates of smoking persist amongst low-income populations. This accounts for a significant portion of the mortality gap between rich and poor within wealthy countries.

i Green Tobacco Sickness is a form of nicotine poisoning. It occurs from skin contact with dissolved nicotine when handling wet tobacco leaves. Its symptoms include nausea, vomiting, stomach cramps, headaches, breathing difficulties, dizziness and fluctuations in blood pressure and heart rate.

The industry has gone out in search of new markets, including minorities, women ('You've Come a Long Way Baby' – Virginia Slims) and adolescents (more children recognize the Camel cartoon than Mickey Mouse). Tobacco giant RJ Reynolds even said: 'African-Americans, Hispanics and women comprise a significant percentage of RJR's business. To ignore their business – only featuring white males in our advertising and only manufacturing styles white males prefer – would leave us open to criticism for racism and sexism, and rightly so.'[4]

Brands designed to appeal to women include the slim cigarettes combining conventions of femininity with notions of emancipation. 'Low tar' brands target women's supposedly more health-conscious nature. Health advocates compare smoking 'light' cigarettes to jumping from the 10th floor instead of the 20th. British American Tobacco (BAT), as far back as 1978, conceded: 'There is now sufficient evidence to challenge the advice to change to a lower delivery [nicotine] brand... smokers will in fact increase the amounts of tar and gas phase they will take in, in order to take in the same amount of nicotine.'[5]

Six years after the introduction of brands marketed to women there was a 110-per-cent increase in the rate of smoking initiation among 12-year-old girls.[6] In industrialized countries where women have been targeted for some time, the death rates from smoking-related diseases are increasing dramatically, responsible for about 30 per cent of all middle-aged female deaths.[7] Additional risks to women include infertility, premature labor, cancer of the cervix and osteoporosis. Smoking while on oral contraceptives is associated with a ten-fold increase in heart disease.

On top of all this, women in the industry are particularly vulnerable through the work they do as farm and leaf factory labor, often for starvation wages. In rural areas, women suffer the brunt of tobacco-related deforestation, often having to walk much further in search of firewood. They also have less access to health information, services and cessation programs.

Preying on the young

A 1981 industry report to Philip Morris (now Altria) observes: 'The overwhelming majority of smokers first begin to smoke while still in their teens... The smoking patterns of teenagers are particularly important to Philip Morris.'[8] While industry denies it, marketing ploys like the 'Camel man' cartoon confirm the extent to which companies aggressively target youth.

Aspirational marketing has been an industry trade mark. Adverts associate smoking with glamor, success, rebellion and independence. Cigarettes are equated with sporting excellence (try sprinting with emphysema) and sexual prowess (smoking causes impotence). The industry has been nothing if not inventive: advertising restrictions or banning resulted in sports sponsorships. When that space closed, Big Tobacco went for 'brand stretching' including labeling of fashionable clothing and accessories and branded cafés. Sponsoring mega-music stars' concerts (as Salem did with Madonna) and then repackaging branded events for TV gets around mass media bans *and* also gets around the world. Industry organizes trendy parties where free cigarettes are handed out. The trade is also diversifying into alternatives such as snuff, water pipes, and *snus* (a moist nicotine powder usually placed under the upper lip for maximum absorption), disingenuously passing them off as 'harm-reduced'.

Exporting death

The tobacco industry is aggressively targeting the untapped markets of low-income countries and 'countries in transition'. By 2030, 70 per cent of all tobacco-related deaths will be in low- and middle-income countries, the figure having increased already by around 64 per cent between 1970 and 1990. With some notable exceptions, there are fewer restrictions on advertising and less public awareness on the dangers of smoking in much of the Majority World. This makes it fertile ground for market expansion.

While 10 years ago only half the world's market was open to transnationals, today the world is their oyster. The South also provides a cheap source of labor (including children) for tobacco production. Most of this today occurs in Southern countries. Philip Morris (now Altria), BAT (British American Tobacco) and RJ Reynolds (Japan Tobacco) own or lease plants in at least 50 countries. Their combined revenue in 1997 was more than $65 billion – greater than the GDP at that date of Costa Rica, Lithuania, Senegal, Sri Lanka, Uganda and Zimbabwe combined. China opened up its vast market in 1998 in exchange for admission into the WTO. Mergers and acquisitions, aided by IMF and World Bank policies encouraging the sale of state monopoly companies, have consolidated about 75 per cent of the world's tobacco market in the hands of the above three companies plus China National Tobacco Corporation (by virtue of its large local market).

Trade liberalization, transnational marketing and the international movement of contraband and counterfeit cigarettes make it hard to control the industry. Many trade agreements restrict industry regulation, while making it easier to trade in tobacco products and facilitating greater competition (see 'WTO vs tobacco control', in Chapter 2). These agreements lead to lower prices and more advertising, both resulting in greater consumption. Singapore's advertising bans have been undermined by cross border 'leakages' from electronic media in Malaysia. Sweden had to compromise on its health warnings as part of the consolidation of the EU.[9]

Stubbing it out

If tobacco were to come onto the market today, it would be banned outright, like cocaine or heroin.

Non-communicable 'pandemics'

Tobacco CEOs would be hunted down like Colombian drug-lords. However, the powerful lobby wields tremendous political influence, allowing it to flourish. Tobacco control advocates in the North and South have had a Herculean task countering this but have made important strides. There has been networking between countries to share expertise, assist in litigation actions and counter trade disputes. Benchmark tobacco control policies have been adopted with countries such as South Africa, Brazil, Thailand and Poland at the forefront. But globalization has eroded many of these hard-won gains.

WHO's Framework Convention on Tobacco Control (FCTC) is a global effort to control a globalizing threat. It was born out of a realization that country-level approaches to address the problem had become insufficient. Transnationals require transnational regulation.[10] The FCTC was WHO's first-ever international treaty and involved a massive global collaboration between academics, public health activists, civil society, and governments. It came into force in 2005 as the most widely embraced international treaty in UN history. Ratified by over 40 countries, it binds them legally to undertake specific tobacco control measures. These include price-hikes and taxes to reduce demand, measures to protect the public from secondary exposure, controls on cigarette content, bans on in-country and cross-border advertising, promotion and sponsorships.

Other measures include prohibitions on labeling of products as 'light' or 'mild', regulation of health warning labels and content disclosures on boxes. FCTC also deals with illicit trade in tobacco products, sales to and by minors and the provision of support for economically viable alternative activities for tobacco workers, growers and individual sellers. All these interventions have been proven to be successful, cost-effective and do-able. Without such comprehensive action, it is estimated that about 1 billion people would be killed by tobacco in the 21st century.

Industry cried foul on a number of FCTC 'articles', saying that 'clean air laws' are bad for all business and tourism and that price hikes will increase smuggling. It also argues that controls could hurt economies and more especially farmers and laborers. The FCTC recognizes the need for technical and financial assistance to support alternatives. Nevertheless, there is evidence showing that the impact on total employment in most countries would be minimal – if anything at all – should consumption fall. The same money would still be spent, but just not on tobacco. The shift to other goods and services would generate new jobs in these sectors.

In a climate where global trade agreements place profits above health, the FCTC is another UN watershed. The *Global Health Watch* publication points to some of FCTC's key victories: it sets precedents for global regulation of an industry and for international cooperation; it gives governments the right to put the health of their citizens above commerce and it will make it easier for governments to pass tobacco control legislation. It advances corporate accountability and bars the industry from involvement in public health policy-making. It also affirms the indispensable role of civil society in international policy-making.[11]

But there is much work to be done still in translating the FCTC into action. And there is the need for constant vigilance: barely a month after Mexico ratified the Convention, Altria and BAT reached an agreement with the Government, effectively preventing it banning tobacco or increasing taxes in exchange for industry payments into a health fund.[12] The industry is upping its corporate social responsibility programs to look good and is investing in 'reduced risk' options and brand-stretching product promotion to by-pass legislation. So, while the FCTC is a major victory, the battle is not yet over. By contrast, the fight against the fast food industry has only just begun.

We reap what eat

Obesity is on the rise in both the North and the South. WHO estimates that in 2005, 300 million people were obese and over 1 billion were overweight. Costs to economies tally into the billions. Childhood obesity is on the up and is responsible for the alarming increase in the number of young people suffering from a range of diseases including heart disease, asthma, metabolic syndrome, tooth decay, depression, hypertension and diabetes. With at least 155 million school-age children worldwide classified as overweight, 30-45 million of whom are considered obese, understanding what is driving this 'emerging pandemic' is vital.[13]

There are many contributing factors such as genetics, culture, social environments and, in the South, the increasing import of Western lifestyles. But a growing body of evidence fingers the food (particularly the fast food) and soft drinks industries. Their products are extremely high in sugar, calories, saturated fat, trans-fatty acids and sodium (salt). In 1987, Americans spent more than $100 billion on fast food, more than they did on higher education, personal computers, software or new cars.[14] With the globalizing food industry, fast and processed food is becoming ubiquitous in the South – sadly even in countries such as China which have excellent 'fast' but nutritious cuisines of their own.

As with tobacco, the US's food and beverage lobby wields significant influence over politicians. The industry spends billions of dollars in manipulative advertising and political influence to dilute government advice and hamper its regulatory power. This includes getting cozy with professional nutrition organizations, funding and publishing industry-favorable nutrition research and sponsoring journals and conferences to influence health professionals. As a result one could be forgiven for thinking that sweets are essential to a healthy diet.

Marian Nestle, nutrition expert and former editor of the 1988 US Surgeon General's Report on Nutrition and Health, says she was instructed that: 'No matter what the research indicated, the Surgeon General's Report could not recommend "eat less meat" as a way to reduce intake of saturated fat, or restrictions on intake of "any other food"'. She added: 'In the industry-friendly climate of the Reagan administration, the producers of foods that might be affected by such advice would complain to their beneficiaries in Congress, and the Report would never be published... Whereas "eat less beef" called the industry to arms, "eat less saturated fat" did not. "Eat less sugar" sent sugar producers to Congress but that industry could live with "choose a diet moderate in sugar"'.[15] When the Report was released it suggested 'limitations on sugar intake only for people particularly vulnerable to dental cavities'. The Surgeon General's Reports on Dietary Fat and Health were totally abandoned in the election year of 2000.

In 2002, the US Sugar Association, together with six other big food industry groups including Coca-Cola and PepsiCo, wrote to the US health secretary, Tommy Thompson, asking him to use his influence to get a WHO report on diet and nutrition withdrawn. The report recommended sugar should account for no more than 10 per cent of a healthy diet. The Association also wrote to WHO's Director General threatening to 'exercise every avenue available to expose the dubious nature' of WHO's report, including attempting to get its $406 million funding from the US cut.[16]

Food companies in 2000 generated nearly $900 billion in sales. They spend over $30 billion on direct advertising and promotions in the US alone.[17] As with tobacco, the industry markets aggressively to minorities and low-income populations in wealthier countries and increasingly to everyone in the Majority World. Trade agreements pave the way for transnational operations. McDonald's operates about 23,000 restaurants worldwide and opens roughly 2,000 new ones per year; there are over 7,000 in Asia. Today Mexicans drink more Coke than milk.[18]

Overweight kids – obese adults

Overweight children are more likely to be overweight adults and advertising to children is believed to be responsible in large part for the growing obesity problem in the North. Given that children in the US 'spend more time consuming media than doing anything else besides sleeping' there is cause for concern.[19] It is estimated that the typical child there sees about 40,000 ads a year on TV alone. This number has doubled since the 1970s, in parallel with the rise in childhood obesity.[20] Given that media is globalizing, this is another cause for concern.

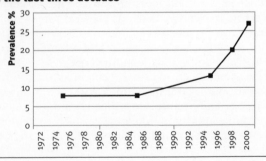

Obesity is skyrocketing

Fast-food consumption is a major contributor to childhood obesity. Kelly Bronwell, Yale University obesity and nutrition expert, calls for stronger policy measures: 'We take Joe Camel off the billboard because it is marketing bad products to our children, but Ronald McDonald is considered cute. How different are they really in their impact, in what they are trying to get kids to do?'

Overweight children – British trends in the last three decades

IOTF www.iotf.org/images/childtrends.jpg

Corporate America spends around $12 billion a year on advertising aimed specifically at children. 'Pester power' is known to influence what caregivers purchase. One US study estimates that the average child viewer may be exposed to one food commercial every five minutes, with 11 food commercials per hour during children's Saturday morning TV programming.[21] Most adverts are for candy, sugar-laden cereals and fast foods empty in calories and high in fat, salt and sugar. Studies show that children under eight years of age interpret adverts as information or entertainment. Pre-schoolers even see them as a continuation of the show being viewed.[22] Young children have also been shown to equate labels like 'diet' and 'fat-free' with 'nutritious'.

Ronald's reach

Cross-promotional marketing entices children into fast food outlets using popular characters or celebrities from blockbuster movies. In 1996, McDonald's and Disney signed a 10-year exclusive global marketing agreement to cross-promote Disney-inspired merchandise with McDonald's restaurants. Product placement with movie characters eating Big Macs abound. A survey of American schoolchildren found that the only fictional character with a higher degree of recognition than Ronald McDonald (who had 96 per cent recognition), was Santa Claus.[23]

McDonald's also has joint promotions with the National Basketball Association and the Olympics; Burger King with the children's network Nickelodeon.

Even classrooms are a marketing opportunity. Channel One, a media initiative reaching around 8 million students in 12,000 US schools, has a deal to provide resource-strapped schools with communications technology in exchange for opportunities to broadcast to a captive audience. While much of the content may be educational, Channel One includes advert breaks on equipment which does not allow for channel-switching, fast-forwarding or volume control. Research has shown that even the two minutes of daily advertising through Channel One exposes young people to fast foods, candy, soft drinks, chips and snacks in seven out of ten commercial breaks.[24]

Between a rock candy and a hard place

Fast foods are increasingly available through US school cafeterias and vending machines. Both private and state schools always need money, wherever they are, and accepting vending machines for snacks and drinks is seen as a reasonable way to generate funds by some school boards.

In many instances the industry is a principal source of income for schools, helping to pay for around $100,000-worth of computer centers, teacher training and other activities per school per year. State and federal law requires schools to switch off vending machines during lunchtime, but some contracts make it clear that they will lose out on their otherwise guaranteed commission if they dare do so. Schools are also signing exclusive deals. One school district apparently signed a 10-year contract worth $1.75 million giving Coke exclusive rights to its schools.

Communities are fighting back. In Philadelphia, NY, parents blocked a $43 million deal between the school system and Coca-Cola by bringing a class-action lawsuit against the Board of Education.

Beyond messing with eating habits, the fast food industry contributes to ill-health by paying low wages – the only Americans who earn lower wages than fast food workers are migrant farmworkers. Decentralized hiring practices and high staff turnover rates have also reduced unionization efforts.

Don't be duped

With increasing bad rap in the press along with attempts at regulation, the food industry has hit back. McDonald's launched 'happy meals' as part of a worldwide campaign to promote 'healthy' eating to children. PepsiCo has committed to 50 per cent of new product revenues coming from its healthful branded product category. It has replaced fried Cheetos with a baked, lower fat version and limited snack serving sizes for all brands. Many question the health value of the new products – some of the combinations still contain more than the daily quota of sugar and salt for young children. And will kids ever choose these less unhealthy options over the familiar favorites that still dominate the menu? Kraft and PepsiCo both report strong growth trends for the healthier products, so perhaps there is some cause for optimism. But critics say the 'healthy options' are simply delaying legislation and litigation, which are seen to be more effective action.

Fix the feeding frenzy

Tactics for changing the situation range from making better food more affordable and accessible, legislative restrictions or outright bans on any form of 'nutrient-challenged' food and beverage promotion to children. Some countries such as Sweden and the Quebec province of Canada have banned such advertising to children on TV. Britain is currently developing restrictions. As parents we can curb the time children spend glued to the TV. We can urge the authorities to better resource schools and to stop the sale of candy, soft drinks and fatty foods: Belgium, France and Portugal have banned junk food marketing at schools entirely. 'Super-size' portions are out because they give people far too much fat, salt, sugar and calories in a dose and of course people tend to eat more if they are given more.

Away from the table, we need to build environments with sidewalks and places to play and exercise. We have to boost the number of local healthy food retailing outlets to invest both in communities' economy and in their health. Even a 'fat' tax on unhealthy foods, earmarking funds for nutrition and recreation has been suggested. Many countries require packaged foods to carry nutrition labels. In 2006 the US extended the existing requirements to include the proportion of harmful trans-fatty acids. According to the Harvard *Public Health Review*, it took 'a small army of researchers on two continents, working for nearly 50 years, as well as vigorous lobbying by health and consumer education groups' just to win this one inclusion. The US regulator, the Food and Drug Administration, believes this change will save an estimated $900 million to $1.8 billion a year in medical costs, lost productivity, pain and suffering.

Ironically, while contributing to obesity, the food and agricultural transnationals are simultaneously deepening global warming, poverty and undernutrition. McDonald's for instance has cut down vast tracts of the world's rainforests for cattle farming land, and agricultural practices of big business are contributing to climate change (see Chapter 5). As seen in chapters 1 and 2, globalizing agribusiness has major health impacts. As a result, interventions to address starvation and obesity must also be tackled in the arena of international trade agreements.

This chapter has looked at two of the key industries implicated in the non-communicable disease pandemic. There are others. The alcohol industry for example is responsible for 4 per cent of the global burden of disease. As well as heart disease and other well known consequences, alcohol is also behind the enormous toll of unintentional and intentional injuries, from car crashes to homicide.

Despite the fact that non-communicable diseases are the major cause of death in most countries, and that overcoming them is essential to the reduction of poverty, there is no mention of them in the MDGs (see Chapter 7). This may well lower the priority they are given on the global agenda. The omission will also allow big business to continue to impede development by putting profits before people.

1 J Sweeny, 'Selling Cigarettes to the Africans', *The Independent* magazine, 29/10/1988, in D Yach, H Wipfli, et al. 'Globalization and Tobacco', *Globalization and Health* (OUP). **2** *Tobacco and the Rights of the Child* Report. WHO, 2001. **3** H Barnum, 'The Economic Burden of the Global Trade in Tobacco', 9th World Conference on Tobacco and Health, October 1994. **4** RJ Reynolds, 'Public Statement on Marketing to Minorities', 1990. RJR, 5077717536-7538, Tobacco Resolution). www.ash.org.uk/html/conduct/html/tobexpld8.html **5** 'Big Tobacco and Women... What the Tobacco Industry's Confidential Documents Reveal', Ash Report, 1998. www.ash.org.uk/html/conduct/html/tobexpld8.html **6** US Dept of Health and Human Services, 'Preventing Tobacco Use Among Young People: A Report of the Surgeon General', Atlanta, GA: Public Health Service, CDC, 1994, in 'Women and Tobacco: Global Trends', www.tobaccofreekids.org/campaign/global. **7** *Tobacco and the Rights of the Child* Report. WHO, 2001. **8** *Tobacco and the Rights of the Child* Report, op. cit. **9** D Yach, op. cit. **10** D Yach, op. cit **11** *Global Health Watch: 2005-2006 Report*, Global Health Watch (Zed Books 2005). **12** K Mulvey, TWN, June 2006, www.twnside.org.sg **13** 'Obesity in Children and Young People: A Crisis in Public Health', International Obesity TaskForce Report, *Obesity Reviews*. www.iotf.org/childhoodobesity.asp). **14** E Schlosser, 'Fast Food Nation: The True Cost of America's Diet', *Rolling Stone* (USA) Issue 794, 3 Sept 1998. **15** M Nestle, *Food Politics*, (University of California Press 2002). **16** S Boseley, 'Sugar Industry Threatens to Scupper WHO', The Guardian (UK), 21 April 2003. **17** M Nestle, MF Jacobsen, 'Halting the Obesity Epidemic: A Public Health Approach', *Public Health Reports*, 115:12-21. 2001, in *Global Health Watch*, op. cit. **18** MF Jacobsen, 2000, 'Liquid Candy: How Soft Drinks are Harming Americans' Health'. Washington DC, Centre for Science in the Public Interest, in *Global Health Watch*, op. cit. **19** D Roberts, U Foehr, *Kids & Media in America* (Cambridge, MA, University Press 2004). **20** D Kunkel, 'Children and Television Advertising', in D Singer, J Singer, (eds) *Handbook of Children and the Media* (Thousands Oaks, Sage 2001) **21** K Kotz, M Story, 'Food Advertisements during Children's Saturday Morning Television Programming: Are They Consistent with Dietary Recommendations?' *Journal of the American Dietetic Association* 94(1994)11:1296-1300. **22** D Kunkel, et al, op.cit. **23** E Schlosser, op. cit **24** J Brand, B Greenberg, 'Commercials in the Classroom: The Impact of Channel One Advertising', *Journal of Advertising Research* 34(1994):18-23.

7 The Big Fix

*'When I give food to the poor, they call me a
saint. When I ask why the poor have no food, they
call me a communist.'*

Dom Hélder Câmara,
Archbishop of Olinda and Recife, Brazil.

**While the world's health problems are big, they
are not insurmountable. If the world commits, we
can fix it. But for change to be sustained, we must
go upstream to where the power lies – internationally, nationally, in the community as well as in the
home.**

IF THE WORLD remains committed to the Universal
Declaration of Human Rights, then 'Health for All' is
the vision we must aspire to. At the core of this vision
is the right to social and economic justice, which means
focusing on 'equity'. Inequities are differences that are
at their core unjust. Achieving health equity means
allocating the most resources to those who are worst
off to ensure that their lives improve at a faster pace.

There are many opinions on how to achieve this.
Ironically, the dominant view – that an unfettered free-
market will do the trick – is the one that has shown to
be the least able to deliver. On the contrary, neo-liberal
macro-economic policies are exacerbating inequity.

The dramatic health gains of the 20th century should
benefit everyone. We do not have all the answers
but we have many. We know that the enormous
suffering caused by largely preventable diseases can be
addressed, often at low cost, through a combination
of socio-economic and health policy measures together
with public health and medical interventions.[1] Cuba,
Sri Lanka, Costa Rica and Kerala state in India show
it can be done, even in the absence of growth and with
relatively little financial investment.

It can be done

In Thailand, Malaysia and Sri Lanka family planning services were embedded within an expanding primary health care system which incorporated trained midwives. Pro-equity policies and services advancing girls' education and women's status more generally were also instituted, particularly in Malaysia and Sri Lanka. These have all resulted in remarkable impacts on fertility, maternal and child mortality.

Maternal mortality since the 1960s in Malaysia, Sri Lanka and Thailand

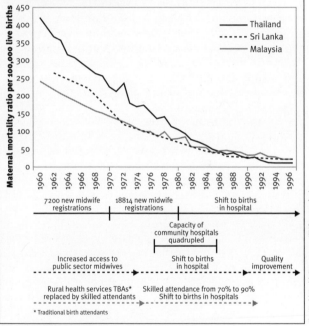

The World Health Report 2005, WHO www.who.int

The Millennium Development Goals (MDG) – the half monty?

The MDGs are a set of eight global mega-goals to be achieved by 2015. They were agreed upon by UN member states in 2000 and have been praised for focusing our collective efforts. They have also been

---

Millennium Development Goals (MDGs)

1: Eradicate extreme poverty and hunger
2: Achieve universal primary education
3: Promote gender equality and empower women
4: Reduce child mortality
5: Improve maternal health
6: Combat HIV/AIDS, malaria, and other diseases
7: Ensure environmental sustainability
8: Develop a global partnership for development

---

criticized as more of the same top-down, vertical approach that has dogged development. Many see glaring gaps. There is no Goal on demilitarization and disarmament, nothing on non-communicable diseases and no substantial focus on changing the rules of the free-market. Despite all the pledges made to women at the 1995 Beijing Conference, a specific goal on sexual and reproductive rights fell off the table and this may jeopardize all the others. While the Goal to empower women looks good, its target is reduced to the elimination of gender disparities in education and undermines the commitment to factor gender equity into all policy. With global resources geared towards the MDGs, other concerns may be neglected. Steven Sinding of the International Planned Parenthood Federation summed it up in this way: 'If you're not a line item, you're out of the game'.[2]

Many push for the Goals to be pro-equity, not simply pro-poor. A goal such as 'Reduce... the under-5 mortality rate' would be made equity sensitive by adding 'ensuring *faster* progress among the poor and other marginalized groups'.[3]

Already UNDP's 2003 *Human Development Report* conceded that 'Women, rural inhabitants, ethnic minorities and other poor people are typically progressing slower than national averages – or showing no progress – even where countries as a whole are moving towards the Goals'.

The UN has expressed concerns that in setting out terms for assistance and debt relief, the 'IMF's program design has paid almost no systematic attention to the Goals when considering a country's budget or macro-economic framework.' In some cases the IMF/World Bank have actually advised countries not to even consider scaled-up [MDG] plans.[4] For example, according to the UN Millennium Project, 'as a condition for the release of additional funds by the IMF in July 2004, Ghana had to roll back part of an agreed wage increase to registered nurses and other core public servants in order to stay within the wage bill ceiling. Ghana is thus another country in which needed investments in the health system are subordinated to macro-economic targets.'[5] Uganda almost lost a $52 million grant from the Global Fund because this would exceed IMF ceilings.[6] In Mozambique the Clinton Foundation had to persuade the IMF to reduce temporarily restrictions on health sector employment.[7] There are calls for at least health sector expenditures to be exempt from conditionalities.

To meet the MDGs we must go boldly 'upstream' *as well as* 'downstream'. Downstream is giving oral rehydration to stop children dying from diarrhea. This is important but children will continue to get sick and die. Going upstream means asking why poor people do not have water or are forced to pay for it. Downstream is providing microbicides so that women can surreptitiously protect themselves from HIV. Upstream is changing gender power relations. Going upstream means getting to the source.

'Upstream' to the global markets

Regulating the 'free' market is one of the top upstream priorities. Those striving for equity need to understand its lexicon and influence the stage where its rules are set – in the WTO and between governments through regional and bilateral Free Trade Agreements. It means

Go upstream

According to the UN Millennium Project Task Force on Child Health and Maternal Health: 'The chasm between what we know and what we do, between our ability to end poverty, despair and destruction and our timid, often contradictory efforts to do so, lies at the heart of the problem. The targets and indicators set by the Millennium Development Goals (MDGs) are framed in technical, results-oriented terms. But the response cannot be simply a technical one, for the challenge posed by the Goals is deeply and fundamentally political. It is about access to and the distribution of power and resources within and between countries; in the structures of global governance; and in the intimate space of families, households and communities. Until we face up to the fundamental anchoring of health status, health systems and health policy in these dynamics, our seriousness about achieving the Goals can be legitimately questioned.'

challenging the global financial institutions (such as the World Bank and IMF) and Northern countries, who through various forms of 'strings attached' debt relief and development assistance, lubricate the free-market's operations.

A strong state accountable to all its citizens is needed to steer countries towards equity. The commercialization of health into a commodity, rather than a 'non-negotiable right' must be reversed. This is becoming increasingly difficult under neo-liberal macro-economic policies which reduce the state's role and exacerbate inequity. Some believe the whole system should be jettisoned. Others want the rules of the game to be re-written for the global good.

The 2001 Doha Round of WTO negotiations, called the 'development round' because of promises to finally put issues of the South on the agenda, did not deliver. Instead it collapsed with a stalemate over agricultural and export subsidies. Irritated by these obstacles, countries are focusing on bilateral and regional negotiations. It is here where much of the scary stuff is now happening and where serious scrutiny needs to intensify.

While it presides, the WTO must reform. Strong-arm and exclusionary tactics by member countries, which disadvantage and divide the South, have to cease. Transparency and accountability need to prevail in its structures and processes. Many public health regulations are scrutinized by trade ministries to ensure they do not present 'undue barriers to trade'. But there are no health impact assessments on trade agreements. There are growing calls for health ministries to have a place at the negotiating table to ensure that agreements do not supersede the right to health. Fairer trade rules, genuine removal of certain public goods and services from the ambit of trade agreements and an independent body to preside over issues of intellectual property rights would be good places to start.

Already, alternatives to TRIPS as a means to incentivize R&D on lifesaving technologies are being explored. There are calls for 'social clauses' in international trade agreements that permit trade sanctions against countries that violate human and labor rights, although there has been mixed reception for this from both the North and the South.[8] Another suggestion is for countries to be exempt from compliance with trade agreements if this compliance will jeopardize their ability to achieve the MDGs.

In addition, mechanisms to better regulate corporations and hold them to account must be devised and implemented.

Get the money to where it is needed
Although there are many competing needs, there is enough money in the world to uplift all people from poverty and to address most major health problems. But there are barriers to getting the money to where it is needed.

Obstacles include political and economic mismanagement in certain countries. In many instances corrupt, oppressive or weak governments are failing

The Big Fix

Regulate industry: General Motors takes the 'car' out of 'caring'

The following formula was used by General Motors (GM) to decide if it was worth fixing a life-threatening design flaw in certain car models. Law suits were already coming in.

$$\frac{500 \text{ fatalities} \times \$200,000/\text{fatality}}{41,000,000 \text{ automobiles}} = \$2.40/\text{automobile}$$

In a case of staggering corporate callousness, GM calculated that law suits would cost the company $2.40 per vehicle compared to $8.59 per vehicle extra to make a safer design. GM decided not to change it. Clearly Big Business can't be left to its own devices. Mechanisms are needed to ensure greater accountability and transparency. These should include, among others, full disclosure of lobbying activities and operations, including profits, labor regulation and toxic emissions and environmental impacts at home and abroad. Government's capacity to regulate and civil society's capacity to perform a 'watchdog' function must be strengthened.

Source: J Bakan, *The Corporation: the Pathological Pursuit of Profit and Power* (Constable & Robinson Ltd, 2004)

---

their citizens. With regard to corruption, it takes two to tango. Organizations such as the People's Health Movement (PHM) call on citizens in rich countries to 'monitor the complicity of their own governments and business in sustaining corruption in poor countries'. Ironically, The World Bank's own track record on corruption is also not so squeaky clean.

Some countries of the South have identified the need to address corruption and governance through peer review mechanisms and the strengthening of regional bodies such as the African Union. The PHM also calls for 'more donor investment for publicly accountable legal and regulatory frameworks to monitor corruption'. Conventions such as the OECD Convention on Combating Bribery and the 2003 UN Convention Against Corruption are important initiatives in this fight.

Other barriers are tax evasion and capital flight into off-shore bank accounts that deprive country coffers of billions of dollars annually for development. War is also diverting resources away. World military spending stands at around $1 trillion. Oxfam maintains that the annual spend on arms by countries in the Majority World would enable them to put every child in school and reduce child mortality rates by two-thirds by 2015. In its post-independence civil war, Mozambique's health budget dropped from 11 to 3 per cent. Currently rich world aid is being diverted to fight the 'war on terror'.

Critically, without a reversal in the net flow of capital from the South to the North it is doubtful that there will ever be enough left for development. What Northern countries give the poor world in aid, they take away and more through debt servicing, unequal terms of trade, outflows of private money, speculative foreign investment and other aspects of the global economy. For example, in Benin and Mali, a 3 per cent drop in GDP resulted from depressed market prices as a result of US cotton subsidies. This is more than twice the amount of debt relief they received in 2001.[9] Estimates are that with fairer rules of trade alone, Africa could see $150 billion coming into its coffers every year.[10]

Debt relief – forgiveness or justice?

Many countries spend far more on servicing debt than they do on health. In Tanzania, where 40 per cent of people die before the age of 35, such payments are six times greater than spending on health care. Britain's 'Africa Commission' initiative and others have called for full debt cancellation for poor countries so they can make the necessary investments in health and development to meet the MDGs. Experts say that the $600 billion in debt relief necessary to assist in meeting the development goals for developing countries only amounts to about 1 per cent of the total financial assets ($53 trillion) of the wealthy countries.[11]

In 1996, after years of lobbying by anti-poverty activists, the World Bank, IMF and the Paris Club

What lies upstream?

A variation of an oft told public health story goes like this: a community noticed people drowning in increasing numbers in a nearby river. The residents spent endless hours and dollars rescuing them but people kept drowning. Until one day some people went upstream. They saw that people were being lured into the fast-flowing river with promises of enormous wealth. All they had to do was to survive the rapids. Until this upstream cause was dealt with, no amount of downstream activity would be sufficient to really stem the drowning multitudes. So too with health. Upstream is where the real determinants of disease lie.

(of creditor countries) devised the Highly Indebted Poor Country (HIPC) initiative to assist with debt repayments and more recently allowed for 100 per cent relief on some debts for countries completing the HIPC initiative process.

To qualify, a country must develop a Poverty Reduction Strategy Paper (PRSP) through a broad-based participatory process, with a welcome opportunity for civil society to influence national policy and development planning. Countries have mixed experiences as to how participative this has been. Many believe it has been largely tokenistic, dominated by the donor/IMF/World Bank agenda – which is in large part to liberalize economies. As with SAPs, HIPC conditionalities also come with macro-economic austerity measures.

The World Bank's Independent Evaluation Group found that despite the imposition of an extensive set of economic conditions, countries in the midst of the HIPC program have seen a worsening of their debt. Of great concern is the finding that many countries quickly got back into debt trouble after completing the HIPC program.[12]

HIPC's macro-economic austerity measures also include restrictions on public expenditure which makes it extremely difficult for countries to attain the MDG targets. PRSP processes are now being expected of countries beyond the HIPC ones and are increasingly a condition for Overseas Development Assistance (ODA).

Debt 'forgiveness' is mostly a misnomer. In many instances the 'naughty' parties are former dictators and the banks that knowingly loaned to them. Where alive, these dictators should cough up and the colluding creditors forfeit the right to profit or recover these odious loans. There are suggestions for this process to be independently adjudicated.

Money that has been freed up from debt relief is being put to good use. According to ActionAid, Mozambique was able to offer all children free immunization and Zambia has made health care free in rural areas.

The kindness of strangers

Alongside debt cancellation, there is a need to scale up donor aid.

Donor countries have promised 0.7 per cent of their GDP as assistance to the South but only Denmark, Norway, Sweden, Luxembourg and the Netherlands have made good on it. Many others have actually decreased their contributions. Analysts believe the per capita value of the annual increase necessary to reach the 0.7 per cent target corresponds to roughly a Big Mac per week in Canada, or just over 1.5 Big Macs per week in the United States.[13]

Although the annual amount of ODA spent on health by all developed nations ($10 billion) may seem a lot, according to Medact it is equivalent to the annual amount Europe spends on ice cream.[14]

ODA amounts to approximately $80 billion a year, but in 2005 ActionAid calculated that only one-third of aid is 'real' aid, targeted at reducing poverty. The other two-thirds is 'phantom' aid which includes aid spent by donors on their own international advisors. For example, the aid spent by donors in 2002 on 740 international advisors in Cambodia was $50-70 million – almost as much as the wage bill for the country's entire civil service of 160,000 people.[15] Of all the EU countries, only Britain and Ireland have stopped making aid conditional on recipient countries buying goods and services from donor countries.

For many donor countries giving debt relief, the conditions are that this comes from their ODA. So again ODA decreases in real terms. This is also considered 'phantom aid' and accounted for 19 per cent of the total aid disbursed to Africa between 2000 and 2003.[16]

Aid is a double-edged sword. Although on the one hand it is desperately needed, on the other there is the danger of recipient dependency and the risk of undue donor influence. There are also concerns that donor-funded programs remain separate from national health and development plans and promote more vertical approaches. A number of donors have attempted to address this.

Donors often attach their own set of strings. Some donors set ideological conditions. For example, US funding for HIV/AIDS in many instances will not support projects that promote abortion or engage with sex workers.

Aid may be conditional on market liberalization. It is often conditional on the use of expertise and goods from donor countries and other means of furthering their countries' commercial interests. In the early 1980s in Mozambique much aid came in the form of drugs and undermined the country's internationally respected program for universal provision of essential medicines. Donor countries insisted that procurement should take place in the donor country. In some instances donated drugs had expired, were not on its essential drug list, had informational inserts in foreign languages and in extreme cases were dangerous and banned in other countries.[17]

In recent times, donor countries are throwing their weight behind Public-Private-Initiatives (PPIs) which have come to dominate much of the health landscape. While these have many detractors, they are undeniably players in the game. Many see PPIs as an important development tool, particularly around accelerating universal access to health technologies. PPIs have however been criticized for their lack of accountability, potential conflict of interests, and the shift of resources away from more integrated, systemic solutions to health problems. With enormous donations from philanthropic institutions such as the Bill and Melinda Gates Foundation, concerns are also raised around the ability of PPIs to skew the global health agenda (see Chapter 3).

For any form of aid to be effective some general principles apply. It must be long-term and assured, making health planning more realistic. It needs to be aligned with country priorities and delinked from conditionalities. There should be accountability and transparency and every attempt made to use local capacity where it exists and to build it where it is lacking.

Restoring health systems

Another 'upstream' issue concerns the public health sector, which in many countries is on the verge of collapse. Under-resourced, unaccountable and poor quality services are unhelpful to both patient and health worker alike. Market-driven reform is a major contributor to the crisis, with liberalizing economies resulting in a weakened state and an unregulated private sector. Yet a strong public health sector with an emphasis on PHC is essential to meet the MDGs.

Estimates of the cost of essential health services range between $34 and $60 per person per year. Most Majority World countries spend only between $1 and $10 and a large proportion of this is paid by poorer people directly. Health care in many countries consumes most of the household budget. According to WHO, serious illness pushes about 100 million people into poverty each year. Oxfam reports that in Zambia, where almost 60 per cent of the population lives on a monthly income of less than $18, it costs $8-10 to treat one episode of pneumonia.

There are three different sources of health financing: government (through tax revenues and compulsory social health insurance with contributions from all employed); private sources (prepayment schemes, private insurance contributions and out-of-pocket payments); and donor funding. Systems are judged on their ability to generate income and deliver on efficiency and equity. While there are pros and cons with most of these, user-fees – the method operating in most poor countries – is the least desirable and should be abolished. Countries most successful in providing

Determinants of health – a multi-level framework for analysis

Individual	Household	Community	National	International
Biology; genetic; age; education; employment; decision-making power	Socio-economic status of household within the community; household access to resources	Level of development; urban vs rural; presence of health resources; gender and other social norms	Country size; population; level of development; type of governance; structure of health system; dependency on global market; nature of health policies; status of women; contours of health sector reform packages	Global economic scenario and dominant economic ideologies; balance of power between various geo-political forces; health sector reform; international human rights regime

Source: adapted from J Cottingham et al, 'Transforming Health Systems: Gender and Rights in Reproductive Health', WHO, 2001.

universal coverage do so through taxation with some form of cross-subsidization (between rich and poor) and risk-pooling (where the well subsidize the sick). Sri Lanka, for example, succeeded through publicly financed public services, free at point-of-delivery.

Countries need to devote more to their health budgets and some can already do this through tax revenue. In 2001 in Abuja, 53 African Union member states agreed to commit at least 15 per cent of their national budgets to health. This is yet to happen.

The *Global Health Watch* publication calls for countries to raise the level of tax revenue to at least 20 per cent of GDP and for public health expenditure (from government and donors) to be at least 5 per cent of GDP. But even with increased ODA and debt cancellation, a country will have to find more sustainable mechanisms to channel money into its coffers. Much of the Majority World depends on tariffs as a source of tax revenue yet trade liberalization is shrinking this vital source. The push to institute competitive taxation to attract foreign investment is also doing the same.[18] With an enabling economic and political environment many governments would have more resources for development.

Other sources of revenue have also been suggested. These include taxes on international currency flows, airlines tax, environmental and arms trade taxes. These, together with demilitarization, could raise significant revenue for development and ensure greater redistribution of wealth. But where is the will?

Flight of human capital

Lack of investment is in part behind the loss of health personnel out of the public sector. Many move to the more lucrative private sector and with liberalization of labor markets, others are heading North. With a shortage of over 4 million health workers worldwide, the problem has reached crisis levels in Latin America and sub-Saharan Africa. In Britain the doctor to

'Working Together for Health', *The World Health Report 2006*, WHO www.who.int

Fleeing the 'coup'

Hospitals and nursing homes in most Western countries and in Australasia would grind to a halt were it not for the three million workers they have recruited from the South. Ironically, in part due to this brain drain, services in the South are grinding to a halt.

Distribution of health workers by level of health expenditure and burden of disease, by WHO region

population ratio is about 1:400, compared to 1:75,000 in Malawi; WHO's standard is 1:1,000.[19]

Many are fleeing wars and poor working conditions. Some, understandably, want better research or advanced training opportunities which are less available in South. It is a vicious cycle. Flight from deteriorating services further damages those services. With aggressive recruitment particularly from the Middle East, Britain and North America and promises of better salaries and working conditions, it is hard not to pack up and go. Some countries are losing 15-40 per cent of their personnel annually; for instance today there are more Ethiopian doctors in Washington DC than in the whole of Ethiopia. Some 40 per cent of nurses and over 30 per cent of doctors entering the British health system were trained abroad. Rich countries save an average of $184,000 in training costs for each recruit. The South invests $500 million annually in training health-care professionals.[20] This amount is equivalent to roughly 25 per cent of the total ODA that developing countries receive for health.[21]

Governments are attempting to regulate this dire situation through bilateral agreements that temper recruitment and strengthen reciprocity. But without better human resource management, decent pay and working conditions, personnel will continue to flee. Tragically, in addition, many health workers are dying of AIDS and other communicable diseases.

Strengthening the state and civil society

Macro-economic reforms that reduce the state in favor of the private sector greatly damage Majority World countries. A weakened state cannot deliver the infrastructure and services necessary to grow the economy. It cannot institute pro-equity policies. It cannot deal with corruption and, if contracting out services to the private sector, it cannot regulate and ensure quality. It cannot regulate unaccountable industries. It cannot provide the stewardship necessary to harness private sector involvement to serve the public good and prevent harmful fragmentation of the health sector.

The state's ability to determine its own development agenda is severely compromised and it will continue to be pulled from pillar to post by international donors, financial institutions, and the globalizing economy which wants it to wither away. A weakened state cannot fulfill its commitments to deliver on the rights of all its citizens. This all assumes of course, good governance on the part of the state itself.

Non-Governmental Organizations (NGOs) have their own history of shaping government agendas, and have both facilitated and at times undermined genuine community engagement. Many lack accountability and have their own funding imperatives that can shape a country's development agenda. But in many countries they have provided a lifeline of services and have served an important watchdog function. A strong civil society, from grassroots activists and NGOs, to academics, is essential to hold government accountable.

In order for policies and strategies to work, grassroots participation in both their design and implementation is important, as are strong communities that can hold all players to account. This was the sentiment behind the Alma Ata Declaration, but decades later much debate rages around how 'do-able' genuine participation is. Certainly in communities where gross inequities exist, greater control over the health sector by people with power, may perpetuate them, serving vested interests

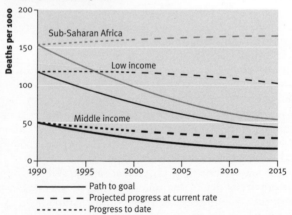

How are we doing?

If current trends continue, most countries on the African continent (where the greatest amount of poverty resides) will not achieve the Millennium Development Goals.

Progress towards Goal 4 – reducing under-5 mortality rate

——— Path to goal
— — — Projected progress at current rate
············ Progress to date

Progress in reducing mortality in children aged under 5 years, comparing sub-Saharan Africa with low and middle income countries in the rest of the world. Solid lines indicate path to goal, dotted lines progress to date, and dashed lines projected progress at current rate.

L Dare, E Buch, 'The Future of Health Care in Africa' *BMJ* 2005;331:1-2 (2 July)

Gender priorities

The UN Millennium Project Task Force on Education and Gender Equality identify seven strategic priorities to ensure MDG* 3 and all other MDGs are met.

1. Meet commitments to universal primary education for girls and strengthen girls' opportunities for post-primary education.
2. Guarantee sexual and reproductive health and rights.
3. Invest in infrastructure (transport, water and sanitation, energy) to reduce women's and girls' time burdens (and free them to 'learn and earn').
4. Guarantee women's and girls' property and inheritance rights.
5. Eliminate gender inequality in employment by decreasing women's reliance on informal employment, closing gender gaps in earnings and reducing occupational segregation.
6. Increase women's share of seats in national parliaments and local government bodies.
7. Combat violence against girls and women.

*Millennium Development Goals

rather than those of the wider community.[22] Women particularly are often excluded from local structures and often benefit the least. But the Alma Ata vision of community participation was a transformative one which stressed equity, and whatever the challenges it is an important goal to pursue.

In today's climate where health is increasingly under siege through various forms of injustice, 'participation' is becoming increasing re-politicized. Activists call for the strengthening of community engagement into collective social movements that have genuine 'transformation' in their sights.

Restoring global governance

If the world has lost its moral compass, who will steer it back on track? We need a system of global governance that acts as the world's conscience, not as its master. Many say for this to happen, the IMF and World Bank must go. Others suggest a return to their original function with no role in global agenda-setting, an end to loan conditionalities; more democratic voting rules, and a leadership appointed on the basis of public accountability (currently, heads are always from the US).

A prerequisite for more equitable distribution of the costs and benefits of globalization is the strengthening of regional political institutions such as the Southern African Development Community (SADC), the African Union (AU) and others. Human rights courts would hold duty bearers to account.

Reform of the UN agencies

Few deny the UN is in need of reform. Under-resourced and increasingly dependent on discretionary funding, it is vulnerable to powerful influences and is often reduced to a 'bit' player. Research reveals how – in attempts to sway opinion in its favor – US aid to member countries increases by about 170 per cent (and a further 53 per cent for the UN) when issues important to its own interests are at stake in the UN Security Council.[23]

WHO seems increasingly beleaguered on the global stage. Variously criticized, along with the UN mothership, as a bloated bureaucracy – 'overly populated with medical professionals' – it is also accused of being too 'disease-focused' and 'a glorified talk-shop'. Other accusations include it being 'impotent', 'servile to Washington' and allowing its agenda to be held to ransom by the rich countries that fund it with private sector interests looking over their shoulders.

Not withstanding these criticisms, WHO has been responsible for significant initiatives which have gone against the dominant grain. Its watershed International Code of Marketing of Breastmilk Substitutes and the Framework Convention on Tobacco Control have taken on two transnational giants. Its Alma Ata vision was a defining event in the history of public health. There are other feathers in its cap.

But many argue that its reputation has been tarnished by its colluding silence in the catastrophic market-driven health sector reforms by the World Bank and IMF and by its support for selective, vertical interventions which undermine its own PHC vision. It is said to have no power to shape the health agenda in a landscape dominated by better resourced, stronger players like the World Bank, IMF and the WTO.[24]

WHO is also seriously criticized for its lack of transparency and accountability. Despite the Alma Ata principles of inclusion, there is no space for public participation in its secret ballot elections. The board itself excludes 160 member states.

Civil society organizations such as the People's Health Movement are calling for sweeping UN reforms to 'ensure they represent the interests of the least powerful'. Enhanced funding and bold moves to populate WHO with a less medical and technocratic staff are also suggested.

'We get what we want, or what we don't refuse' [i 25]

The fight for social and economic justice throughout the world has in many instances invoked the call for 'Health for All', albeit under different banners. Political oppression invariably manifests in cruel health impacts so it is no surprise that over the years liberation struggles have integrated health into their platforms of action. It is fair to say that improvements in health historically come from struggle and the way things are going in the 21st century, it seems likely that it is struggle that will bring about improvements in the future.

The link between health and political activism has been around for centuries. In the 18th century, Eugenio Espejo, a Mestizo physician in colonial Ecuador, saw links between living conditions and smallpox. He integrated his medical work with the fight for socio-political and economic change in Ecuador. Rudolph Virchow, a German physician, made similar links in

i Muhammad Yunus, founder of the Grameen Bank in Bangladesh and Nobel Peace Prize laureate the 19th century. Sent by the Prussian Government to investigate an outbreak of typhus in Silesia, his recommendations were for political freedom, educational and economic reforms. His beliefs influenced the 1848 revolution in which he himself participated.

In the 1900s many of Virchow's followers moved to Latin America and influenced others to 'join the dots'. Today's 'Latin American Social Medicine' movement, which arose during the 1950s, traces its roots back to Virchow.

Salvador Allende, later President of Chile, was deeply affected by Virchow's ideas. He and others in Latin America were also influenced by the public health movement that emerged as part of the Spanish Civil War's fight against fascism. Allende helped shape Chile's national health program which guaranteed universal access to services and was linked to significant socio-economic reforms.

Health activism

Social activism for health in Chile and many other parts of Latin America arose out of workers' collective daily experiences of the impact of poverty and poor working conditions on their health. Health was an integral part of the Cuban revolution. Revolutionary Che Guevara put aside a lucrative career in clinical medicine to heal the root causes of disease. He called on health workers to understand the social origins of medicine and the need for systemic changes to improve health.[26] The struggle for health was also integral to the 1979 Nicaraguan revolution although subsequent reforms in the sector have been controversial. Many Latin American health workers were part of the Liberation Theology Movement in which activism around health was an important tool for social justice. The incorporation of health into these social movements influenced similar trends across the world. Brazilian educator Paulo Freire was also highly influential. His educational methodologies that stimulated a critical consciousness of oppression were later applied to health. In South Africa, health workers were central to the anti-apartheid struggle, inspired also by Latin America as well as early liberation movements and social transformation in other parts of Africa. Because health was so politicized in these conflicts, health workers from Nicaragua to Mozambique were targeted, as were the services they set up.

In industrialized countries social activism and labor movements were also in large part responsible for the improved socio-economic conditions leading to health improvements in the first half of the 20th century. Women's movements have shifted world consciousness around gender.

Civil society activists have partnered academics and scientists to bring about social change. They have pressured governments, for instance to secure universal access to ARVs to treat AIDS. Together they have taken on Big Pharma and influenced the WTO agenda. WHO garnered similar support to craft the landmark Framework Convention for Tobacco Control. Environmental groups have put climate change and sustainable development on the global agenda and landless people's movements the world over have pushed for reform. Anti-poverty coalitions have put the spotlight on the debt crisis. People have united to overthrow oppressive regimes and elected better ones.

On a local level, parents have joined forces to regulate the fast food industry's infiltration into schools. Communities have united to stop the alcohol industry advertising near schools. Consumer concerns took GM foods off the shelves in Britain. Thousands of grassroots organizations around the world work tirelessly to bring about change at community level.

The People's Health Movement formed in 2000 has brought together health workers to put 'Health For All' back onto center stage. Its 'People's Charter for Health' is the most widely endorsed consensus document on health since the Alma Ata Declaration.

The attainment of 'Health for All' is possible if activists form alliances to knock louder on the doors of power. Connectivity is the upside of globalization – as seen in 1999 when 50,000 protesters gathered outside the WTO meeting in Seattle to denounce an economic world order that disregards human rights. Today, people the world over have coalesced into groups which in turn have become global movements. The World Social Forum (WSF), for example, was formed to put social and economic justice on the front burner.

This is no easy task when the prevailing macro-economic order is seen as inevitable. Critics say socialism had its chance and blew it. To suggest (as the WSF does) that 'another world is possible' is labeled naïve. Yet with growing evidence of market failures in the area of health and development, the calls for 'another world' are becoming increasingly mainstream. Ordinary people, tired of being told to pull themselves up by the bootstraps when they don't even have boots, are being joined in their calls by economists, scientists, academics and politicians. They may not all be out on the streets, but many of them are there in spirit. They may not all have exactly the same vision for another world but they all want a more equitable one.

A better world *is* possible. But as Paulo Freire said: 'Hope… does not consist of crossing one's arms and waiting'.[27]

1 'Reducing Risks, Promoting Healthy Life', *World Health Report 2002*, WHO www.who.int **2** B Crossette, 'Reproductive Health and the MDGs: The Missing Link', Population Program of the William and Flora Hewlett Foundation, Dec 2004. **3** UN MP Task Force on Child Health and Maternal Health op. cit. **4** W Waruru, 'IMF, World Bank Come Under Heavy Criticism', The East African Standard (Nairobi, (2005), in P Bond op. cit. **5** UN MP Task Force on Child Health and Maternal Health op. cit. **6** *Global Health Watch: 2005-2006* (Zed Books 2005).**7** E Friedman, 2004. *An Action Plan to Prevent Brain Drain: Building Equitable Health Systems in Africa*. Boston MA: PHR. www.phrusa.org/campaigns/aids/pdf.braindrain.pdf **8** R Labonte, M Sanger, 'Glossary of the WTO and Public Health: Part 2', *J Epi Community Health* 2006;60:738-744. **9** 'Improving Market Access', *Issues Brief*. IMF, 2002 in R

Labonte et. al, *Fatal Indifference: The G8, Africa and Global Health*, (University of Cape Town Press 2004). **10** J Cornish, 'Dissent in the Debt Ranks', *Mail&Guardian* newspaper, June 24-30, 2005. **11** R Labonte et al, *Fatal Indifference: The G8, Africa and Global Health*, (University of Cape Town Press 2004). **12** http://en.civilg8. ru/1861.php **13** R Labonte et al, op. cit. **14** www.medact.org **15** 'Real Aid Reports' Action Aid, 2006.   www.actionaid.org.uk/100473/real_aid.html **16** P Bond, 'A review of Debt, Aid, Trade Relations', *Afrodad Occasional Papers*, Issue#3, Feb 2006. **17** J Cliff, et al, 'Mozambique Health Holding the Line', *Review of African Political Economy* Vol 13 No 36 Summer 1986: pp7-23. **18** R Labonte, et al, op. cit. **19** *Global Health Watch op. cit.* **20** D Frommel, 'Global market in medical workers', *Le Monde Diplomatique*, May 2002, in R Labonte et. al, op. cit. **21** R Labonte, et al, op. cit. **22** UN MP Task Force on Child Health and Maternal Health op. cit. **23** I Kuziemko, E Werker, 'How Much is a Seat on the Security Council Worth? Foreign Aid and Bribery at the UN'. *J Polit Econ* 2006;114:905-30, in D Woodward, *The Lancet*, Vol 369, Jan 6 2007; pp12-13. **24** M Westerhaus, A Castro. 'How Do Intellectual Property Law and International Trade Agreements Affect Access to Antiretroviral Therapy?' PLoS Med 3(8): e332 August 8, 2006. doi:10.1371/journal. pmed.0030332 **25** Latin American examples drawn largely from H Waitzkin, et al. 'Social Medicine Then and Now: Lessons from Latin America', *American Journal of Public Health,* October 2001, Vol 91, No 10. **26** Ernesto 'Che' Guevara, On revolutionary medicine, in: J Gerassi (ed.) *Venceremos! The Speeches and Writings of Ernesto Che Guevara*, (Clarion 1968:112–119), in H Waitzkin, op. cit. **27** P Freire, *Pedagogy of the Oppressed* (Continuum International Publishing Group 1970).

Resources and Contacts

Global Health Watch 2005-2006: An Alternate World Health Report,
(Zed Books 2005).
Globalization and its Discontents, Joseph E. Stiglitz, (Penguin 2002).
Sickness and Wealth: the Corporate Assault on Global Health, Meridith Fort,
Mary Anne Mercer, Oscar Gish, (eds) (South End Press 2004).
The Silent Takeover: Global Capitalism and the Death of Democracy, Noreen
Hertz, (The Free Press 2001).
The Corporation: The Pathological Pursuit of Power and Profit, Joel Bakan,
(Constable & Robinson 2004, 2005).
Food Politics, Marion Nestle, (University of California Press 2002).
*On the Take: How Medicine's Complicity With Big Business Can Endanger Your
Health*, JP Kassirer, (Oxford University Press 2005).
Development as Freedom, Amartya Sen (Anchor Books 1999).
No Logo, Naomi Klein (Flamingo 2000).
The No-Nonsense Guide to Globalization, Wayne Ellwood (New Internationalist/
Verso 2001).
The No-Nonsense Guide to HIV/AIDS, Shereen Usdin (New Internationalist/
Verso 2003).

Global Health Watch: Campaign Agenda 2005-2006
www.ghwatch.org/2005report/GlobalHealthAction0506.pdf

The Global Tobacco Treaty Action Guide
www.stopcorporateabuse.org/cms/page1345.cfm

Health Action International Africa/WHO: *Medicine Prices: A Critical Barrier
to Access; How to Advocate for Implementation of Recommendations from
Medicine Prices Surveys.* www.haiafrica.org/index.php?option=com_content&ta
sk=view&id=176&Itemid=41

Arrow (Asia-Pacific Resource and Research Centre for Women)
www.arrow.org.my

Association Latinoamericana de Medicina Social (ALAMES)
www.socialmedicine.org/alames.html

Canadian Centre for Policy Alternatives
www.policyalternatives.ca

CIVICUS
www.civicus.org

The Cornerhouse
www.thecornerhouse.org.uk

Corporate Accountability International
www.stopcorporateabuse.org

Development Alternatives with Women for a New Era (DAWN)
www.dawnnet.org

EQUINET
www.equinetafrica.org

FAHAMU Networks for Social Justice
www.fahamu.org

Focus on the Global South
www.focusweb.org

The Global Equity Gauge Alliance
www.gega.org.za

Health Global Access Project (GAP)
www.healthgap.org

Health Action International (HAI)
Africa: www.haiafrica.org
Asia-Pacific: www.haiap.org

Health Alliance International
http://depts.washington.edu/haiuw

The Hesperian Foundation
www.hesperian.org

International Institute for Sustainable Development (IISD)
www.iisd.org

Knowledge Ecology International (KEI)
www.cptech.org

Medact
www.medact.org/medact_information.php

Médecins Sans Frontières (MSF)
www.msf.org

The Millennium Project
www.unmillenniumproject.org

New Economics Foundation
www.neweconomics.org

Oxfam
www.oxfam.org

The Pan-African Treatment Access Movement:
www.patam.org

People's Health Movement
www.phmovement.org

Physicians for Human Rights
www.dundee.ac.uk/med&humanrights/SSM/phr/home.html

Physicians for Social Responsibility
www.psr.org

Public Citizen
www.citizen.org

Third World Network (TWN)
www.twnside.org.sg

TWN Africa
www.twnafrica.org

Treatment Action Campaign
www.tac.org.za

WHO
www.who.int/en/

Index

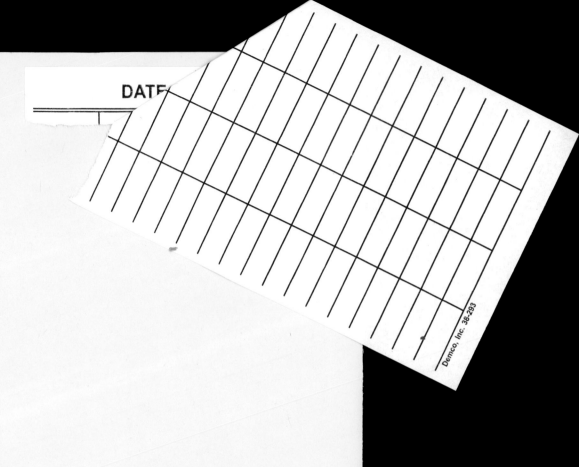

Demco, Inc. 38-293